Darkest Secrets of Negotiation Masters:

How to Protect Yourself, Overcome Intimidation, Get Stronger, and Turn the Power to Good

Tom Marcoux
America's Communication Coach

Book #2 in the nine volume series
Darkest Secrets by Tom Marcoux

A QuickBreakthrough Publishing Edition

QuickBreakthrough Publishing is an imprint of Tom Marcoux Media, LLC. More copies are available from the publisher, Tom Marcoux Media, LLC. Please call (415) 572-6609 or write TomSuperCoach@gmail.com

or visit www.TomSuperCoach.com

or Tom's blog: www.BeHeardandBeTrusted.com

This book was developed and written with care. Names and details were modified to respect privacy.

Disclaimer: The author and publisher acknowledge that each person's situation is unique, and that readers have full responsibility to seek consultations with health, financial, spiritual and legal professionals. The author and publisher make no representations or warranties of any kind, and the author and publisher shall not be liable for any special, consequential or exemplary damages resulting, in whole or in part, from the reader's use of, or reliance upon, this material.:

Other Books by Tom Marcoux:

- Darkest Secrets of Charisma
- Darkest Secrets of Persuasion and Seduction Masters
- Darkest Secrets of Making a Pitch to the Film and Television Industry
- Darkest Secrets of Business Communication: Using Your Personal Brand
- Darkest Secrets of Small Business Marketing
- Darkest Secrets of Spiritual Seduction Masters
- Darkest Secrets of the Film and Television Industry Every Actor Should Know
- Darkest Secrets of Film Directing

CONTENTS

DEDICATION AND ACKNOWLEDGEMENTS

This book is dedicated to the terrific book and film consultant, and author Johanna E. Mac Leod. It is also dedicated to the other team members. Thanks to Danek S. Kaus and Joan Harrison for editing. Thanks to Daniel Buhlman for the book's front cover photography and rendering. Thanks to Johanna E. MacLeod for rendering the back cover for this edition. Thanks for the good times to my father, Al Marcoux. Thanks to my mother, Sumiyo Marcoux, a kind, generous soul. Thanks to Higher Power. Thanks to our readers, audiences, clients, my graduate/college students and my team members of Tom Marcoux Media, LLC.

BOOK I: DARKEST SECRETS OF NEGOTIATION MASTERS

I wasn't going to write this book, but something shocking happened that pushed me to write it—so you could learn how to *protect yourself.*

First, you need to know that for 27 years, I've been dedicated to helping people just like you. I've helped people protect themselves from physical danger. I started by teaching karate, and then swimming—and now communication methods for positive results.

The incident that pushed me to write this book occurred when someone I trusted to work on a deal for me turned against me. He wanted to do the least amount of work and wanted to "force me" to settle for an amount that didn't cover my expenses. How is this shocking? I've worked with this person on various projects, and *I trusted him.* This person wrote certain phrases in letters to me, which pushed me toward certain conclusions (like the negotiation is over; nothing else can be done) and disempowered me. In essence, he was "negotiating hard" and pushing me. (I will cover his dark methods and the countermeasures in the section "Entangle you in paperwork.")

I got angry. But I kept my calm on the outside. While upset, I realized that many people are getting hurt because Dark Negotiators are using techniques to coerce them into making poor decisions.

Now I can serve as your coach. You can learn about and rehearse the methods in this book so you can protect yourself and achieve favorable outcomes during negotiation.

Over the years, I have realized that not only do business people use intimidation and dark negotiation methods, so do some of our own family members. Within a number of paragraphs, I will show you *Countermeasures to 9 Dark Negotiation Methods.*

Before we go further, we must discuss how you can empower yourself.

You Can Turn a Negotiation into a Positive Process
What is negotiation? Some people talk of a negotiation as "a fight with words in which you're trying to defend yourself and then win." They also speak of the other person as "your opponent." This approach is misguided.

The Merriam-Webster Dictionary refers to "negotiation" as "the act or process of conferring with another so as to arrive at the settlement of some matter."

So this source does not define negotiation as "fighting with words." And in light of this, we can turn negotiation into a positive process. How? When necessary, we can calm down and *think of the other person as simply "the other."* When you make a positive connection with that person, you're more likely to negotiate a satisfying result. We avoid the trap of getting furious and considering the other person a villain. If you label the other person as a villain, what does that make you? It could make you a "hero". Or it could make you a "victim." Either way you shut yourself off from a powerful opportunity: *you could turn the other person into an associate.*

For example, I once turned "the other" in negotiation into an associate. It started off badly. This person was the manager of a store that was selling jewelry that was labeled Sterling silver, but it turned my family member's finger green. In essence, the manager was part of an organization that was cheating. Still, I got this manager to give me what I wanted. How? I treated him as "the other" (just another person in front of me). That is, I consciously shifted my thoughts from "opponent" to the possibility of an associate to get the situation resolved. I appealed to his selfish interests. I realized that I could get what I wanted if I helped him get what he wanted. (Further into this book in the section *Remember "It's All Good Practice,"* we go through a breakdown of the whole jewelry store negotiation.)

Now, I'll say something unusual:

Negotiation is often a crisis because it triggers and "floods" you with disempowering feelings.

When I use the phrase "triggers you," I'm talking about how something in the environment can bring up difficult emotions. For example, one of my clients grew up in a family that would yell during heated conversations. Her husband complains that she is "verbally abusive." The word "abusive" is a trigger for her: it reminds her of her father's bullying behavior. Now, she feels provoked, and her conversation with her husband escalates to an argument.

This book includes information from the field of neurology: the study of the brain. Each of us has been given this miracle "machine"—a body with a brain. But we were not issued a user's manual. So, I study every day, reading several books in a year trying to learn more about the human brain and to ensure the methods I convey are based in scientific research.

When I said, "Negotiation is a crisis because it triggers and floods you with disempowering feelings," I was talking about how situations that require negotiation can bring up difficult emotions.

The term "flooded" refers to how people can be overwhelmed by emotion triggered by an event. Some individuals, when flooded, experience a rise in heart rate, sweating and other symptoms of extreme anxiety. Other people, when flooded, emotionally shut down. Some of them become tired and even escape to their bed.

Stress can trigger the "flooded" reaction. UC Irvine stress resilience psychologist Salvatore Maddi discovered that people who do well under stress have the "Three C's": commitment, control and challenge. *This book is designed to help you to employ "The Three C's" when you are in a negotiation.*

Commitment: Resilient people don't avoid stress. They face into it (like facing the wind), maintaining a commitment to stay engaged with the world and to pursue their goals.

Control: Resilient people identify where they have some control in a situation. (Perhaps, they'll use deep breathing to calm down.) They make the most of the details that they control. This is the opposite of people who consider themselves helpless.

Challenge: Resilient people turn a threat (a problem or situation in which they may lose something) into an opportunity to stretch and to grow. They learn and they become stronger.

In essence, when you train yourself to employ the "Three C's," you become resilient and able to think with clarity during a negotiation.

Negotiation is Like Fighting a Fire

How does a fire chief know when to send some fire personnel into an area of a building to perform various duties like break down doors to search for victims or have them retreat to save their own lives?

Psychology researcher Gary Klein decided to study fire fighters to understand optimum ways of dealing with stress. During the course of his research, Klein developed *a model of experience-based intuition with mental simulation.* This model helps us understand how to perform well under intense stress (like during a negotiation). He built this model from interviewing veteran firefighters. Author Taylor Clark summed up the findings in this way: "The elite firefighters had seen so many fires over the years that a web of patterns had been etched into their subconscious mind, lending them incredibly solid instincts."

So I provide methods throughout this book and I invite you to practice these methods (perhaps with a trusted friend). Rehearsing gives you a form of "simulation" — which is somewhat similar to how firepeople train to fight fires using a special training building. Similarly, pilots have regular training in flight simulators. The air travel industry knows that people tend to default to their training when under stress. That's the reason that they require that pilots regularly update their skills while using flight simulators.

You can update your negotiation skills by using this book as your training manual, so in difficult negotiations you will default to this training.

Rehearse with someone with whom you feel safe. Perhaps you can practice with a trusted friend or family member. A number of people seek a coach, counselor or therapist to practice negotiation skills for issues that come up in personal relationships and business interactions.

Overcome Reactions to Negotiation as a Crisis

Human beings tend to react to a crisis in these manners: fight, flight or freeze. What does this look like?

- Fight: A child hit on the shoulder punches back as a reflex.
- Flight: In the animal kingdom, a rabbit runs away

from a bear. (Bears chase running rabbits and running people.)

- Freeze: A deer stops in his tracks when confronted by the headlights of an oncoming car.

Reactions like these can cause bad outcomes for you in a negotiation.

Overcome the "Fight" Reaction

Let's face it. Some of us are more high strung and likely to fight. Perhaps you grew up in a family in which a number of siblings struggled for attention and toys. Or you were pushed around by a schoolyard bully.

People who have endured such incidents are conditioned to go on alert. When conflict shows up, your amygdala and brain stem (known as the emotional brain) go on red alert. Adrenaline and cortisol pump into your bloodstream.

Now the fight reaction is helpful if you're trying to save your life in the wilderness, but the fight reaction can cause you trouble—particularly if you're just defending your ego. That is, you have the physiological reaction as if your life is at risk, when you might only receive a verbal reprimand for an error at work.

The solution is for you to quickly reinterpret the situation. Your life is not at stake. You need to coach yourself in the process of transforming a tendency to react to a decision to respond.

For example, one of my clients, Stephen, who runs a business from home felt a tornado of anxiety rise in his chest. He was going to lose a couple of days of productivity because his girlfriend, Marlena, had misfiled some paperwork.

In a way, Stephen has conditioned himself to be on alert every time he said: "I'm an entrepreneur. I only get paid by what I get done. I don't get paid for just showing up at work and answering a phone." By repeating this phrase, almost like a mantra, Stephen is constantly concerned about "losing time" and "wasting time." He is afraid that he won't earn enough to pay his bills.

Stephen realized that his constant "being on edge" was detrimental to his relationship with Marlena and the business relationships with the contractors he hires for large projects.

To change his reaction to a response, Stephen followed the patterns we instilled in a coaching session. He took the following actions and considered the following questions:
1) He sat down.
2) He took deep breaths.
3) He thought, "What do I really want here?"
4) "Am I really going to get hurt here?"
5) "How can I shift my mind to something else?"
6) "How can I calm down so I don't yell at Marlena and cause damage to my relationship?"
7) He listened to music.
8) He did some other important task.

These combined methods helped Stephen to switch the direction of his thoughts and to improve his mood. He stepped out of the unresourceful emotional state of anxiety and into a more effective state of calm. Being calm helped. He avoided saying angry things to Marlena, and he was able to proceed with his day. Researchers report that each interruption can cause a person to lose 15 minutes of productivity. One way to minimize such a disruption is to practice methods to calm down as quickly as possible.

Overcome the "Flight" Reaction

When faced with some sort of conflict, some people feel like running. Many do; they get up and leave the room. Others emotionally leave the conversation. For example, some years ago, I was at a friend's home. When dinnertime came, the television was still on. In deference to having a guest present, the father turned off the television but the mother looked through a magazine at the dinner table.

I was seeing someone not engaged with her family members (and me, the guest). Why? For one thing, it takes work! In addition, when you engage with a person, you never know if that person will say something that will bring up uncomfortable feelings in you. Then you'll need to demonstrate compassion—and that takes work, too.

So what's the solution?

1) First, open your eyes and observe when you're engaged in "flight" behavior. Have you tuned out? Or have you got up in a huff and left the room?

2) Second, make sure you take care of your personal energy. Get enough sleep, rest, time with friends, quiet time, and more.

3) Third, get coaching and/or practice how to engage with other people. Small talk is "big talk" in disguise. It makes a big difference when you ask people gentle questions and listen. Try questions like:

- How are things going for you?
- What are you looking forward to?
- How can I be supportive of what you're doing?

4) Fourth, learn how to listen and direct your attention to the other person.

For you to be an Effective Negotiator, you need to notice and then deal with your own tendencies related to "emotional flight." The mother reading a magazine at the dinner table was engaging in her own version of emotional flight.

Emotional flight is really tuning out. Human beings can tell when another person has emotionally tuned out. How? Some cognitive scientists theorize that mirror neurons (particular brain cells) are involved. When a human being (or primate) sees an action, certain brain cells are stimulated. This is how a movie works on the audience. We see a film character cry and similar feelings are generated in us.

The big question is: how can an Effective Negotiator build a bridge to the other person?
Building such a bridge is the opposite of emotional flight.

The answer is related to *"Fourth, learn how to listen and direct your attention to the other person."*

The truth is: people have three natural processes that must be overcome so that they can truly listen and direct their attention to the other person. I call the processes: *the 3 Listening Blockers.*

1) Judging

We judge things all the time. "Yes, she's right." "No, he's wrong." The solution is to put our judgment on hold in our mind, and ask a gentle follow-up question.

2) Defending

People say, "No! I don't always forget to take out the garbage. I took it out two times last month!" It takes practice to ask, "Is there anything else?" Instead of cutting off the other person, it helps to ask a couple of questions to help the person complete expressing their feelings.

3) Me, Too—One Up

Imagine the scene: Joe says, exhaustion in his voice, "I'm so tired of losing sleep, staying up with our new son." His friend Margaret replies, "Yes. I can understand. I have three children." At first glance, it seems like Margaret is sympathizing or even empathizing with Joe's situation. But in this example, saying, "I have three children" is like saying, "I'm better than you [one up on you] because I can handle taking care of two more children than you do."

When we "one up," we're turning the spotlight (of the conversation) back upon ourselves. The person is now metaphorically in the dark, and he or she does not like that! When you catch yourself doing "me, too—one up," pause and ask a gentle question. Turn that conversation spotlight back upon the other person.

Overcome the "Freeze" Reaction

To overcome the freeze reaction, you need rehearsal. You

need to condition your brain so that you do not freeze during a crisis. I learned this in an extreme situation. I have never written about this before, but now I believe my story can be helpful to you.

It was 1994 and I walked on Industrial Way in San Carlos, California. I had just attended the graduation ceremony of Kidpower, a self-defense program for children. The nephew and niece of my then-girlfriend had just completed Kidpower's program. To give the audience of assembled parents and friends an experience of what the children learned, the Kidpower leader had the parents and friends yell, "No!" Her intention was for the parents and friends to realize the power of the word "No!" She went on to explain that the children had new tools to help them in a child abduction situation. The youngsters had been trained to say, "No! This is not my father! I need help!"

There is a lot of power in the word No! If you are alone, try it now. Say loudly, "No!" Good.

So, along with the parents, I had learned about the power of using one's voice. It was only twenty seven minutes later when I was confronted with a tough situation. I had stepped away from the graduation ceremony building to get a snack at the local McDonald's. On my way back, walking on Industrial Way, I glanced about. I saw a group of six young men. Their body language and clothing clued me that this was a gang. Some yards away, they moved like a wolf pack on the other side of the street. It was a Sunday. No one was on the street except the gang and me.

They saw me. The terror struck me when they crossed the

street toward me. Industrial Way is double-wide street. It took a long time for them to reach me. My mind was racing, "Do I run?"

They had me surrounded. I looked like a target. Slim, Asian young man wearing a suit, with a shoulder pack, pulling a luggage cart.

Next, I used my body to say, "I will fight." I took my shoulder pack off. I stepped in front of the cart. I breathed in and stood tall.

The gang leader uttered a terrifying threat, like something that might be heard in certain prisons:

"Do you like anal sex?"

"No. Do you?!" I said in a strong, deep voice—several octaves deeper than my normal speaking voice. Everything about me: my voice, facial expression, and body language said, "I will fight."

In a couple of moments, the gang started talking among themselves. And they walked away from me.

I was stunned about the power of my voice and my word choice of "No. Do you?"

I was convinced that day, and to the present, that my training and rehearsal of the word, "No!" had primed me to protect myself. People often become tongue-tied in stressful situations. Being able to say "No" allowed me to complete the phrase "No. Do you?" The body language of the gang informed me that they were gearing up to assault me. But I had responded in a powerful way that presented strength.

I made it back to the building that had housed the Kidpower graduation ceremony. I tracked down one of the instructors and asked about special self-defense training for men. The only class for men was available 400 miles away. I signed up.

[I have helped women gain scholarships to the specialized self-defense training entitled Impact-Model Mugging. I have even trained with the original creator of this unique form of training.]

Negotiation involves body language and tone of voice. The gang leader and gang were looking for an easy victim. My communication conveyed that I was going to fight with all my spirit and that one or more of them would get hurt. It was not worth it to them.

Body language, verbal tone and word choice were necessary in this negotiation.

How was this a negotiation? People were communicating to get what they wanted. The gang wanted a "play thing." And I wanted no trouble. I'm grateful that I gained my objective.

Develop Your Ability to Respond

To respond well to anything that the other does in a negotiation, you need to train your mind to instantaneously have a list of options. The person with more behavioral options can adapt well. This book provides a lot of proven options in four sections (Book I through Book IV):

1) Darkest Secrets of Negotiation Masters
2) Turn Effective Negotiating Power to Good
3) 10 General Principles of Effective Negotiating
4) Use Strategies to Make Yourself Stronger (The Strong Can Negotiate Effectively)

Each negotiation situation is unique. Using a set of principles can help you adapt to the multitude of things you'll be confronted with.

Principle #1:
If you're going into a high-stakes negotiation,
you need to study negotiation methods
like an Olympic athlete studies and practices.

You'll get the most out of this book when you go beyond merely reading it. In fact, I have read this entire book aloud to one of the team members at my company. Why? Because I want to practice the methods, too. Saying things out loud creates more impact as we seek to condition ourselves to be effective at negotiation.

If you say out loud one of the suggested phrases [like: "That's not acceptable. You'll need to do better than that"], you will have actually practiced—as opposed to merely reading this book silently.

Rehearse the methods before you enter a negotiation.

(By the way, I'm really glad that you're reading this book. Years ago, when I entered one of my first business deals, I really could have used a book like this one. So I needed to write it. It's reported that Stephen King writes the books that he wants to read.)

Principle #2:
Make no mistake: The other wants to win

I've noticed that the other often says reassuring words like: "I want to make sure that this is a win-win." Let's face the truth. The other wants to win.

It's advantageous to you to give the other a chance to feel that he or she has won. The way effective negotiation works is that people value different things to varying degrees. For example, people often think that price is the most important detail. However, I have sometimes agreed to a higher price because I was working with someone who I trusted and who would save me time. Time is valuable! And I have valued time over price. People do value different things to varying degrees. For example, I have friends who would go to three stores to find the lowest price. On the other hand, I factor in my time in the car.

How do you help the other feel like he or she has won? When you concede a point (that is, give in and let the other have something he wants), make sure that you make it sound like your concession was a big thing. You can say something like: "Okay. This is tough on me. It's making me really stretch. You win on that. You can have that." Make sure that the other feels like he or she has won. The other will feel better and will be more likely to abide by the terms that were negotiated.

Principle #3:
If your goal is benevolent,

you can eliminate hesitation.

Let's face this now. Many of us hesitate to learn and practice negotiation skills. Why? Some people equate negotiation with manipulation. And many of us equate manipulation with being a bad person. So automatically, some people just want to avoid the whole topic of negotiation.

Right here, right now, I want to emphasize that effective negotiation can be a benevolent process. How? This is an AND world. You can get what you want AND the other can get what he or she wants. How can that occur? Because we want things to differing degrees. For example, many teachers want the fulfillment of helping younger people. And many of them make the decision that they are willing to be paid a lower salary than, let's say, an attorney or a corporate trainer. (Some teachers I know get to the point that they want their life to become less financially tough, so they move on from teaching.)

When I say, If your goal is benevolent, you can eliminate hesitation, I'm talking about your making a choice to avoid hesitating about studying and rehearsing negotiation methods. Many of us do not want to hurt other people. So negotiate in a way that you fulfill your goals and you make sure that the other gains benefits, too.

Principle #4:
Strengthen yourself to be unfazed by the other's extreme tactics.
Realize that you do not need to lower yourself to use dark methods.

As an Effective Negotiator, you will view the whole situation. You'll make sure that you won't loose your cool, and you'll be sure you'll take action to meet your goals and see that the other gains valuable benefits, too. You'll also notice that people use extreme tactics often because they're scared or some extreme tactic is just what they know.

Let's say someone uses the extreme tactic of yelling. You do not need to lower yourself to yell back. When you've strengthened yourself, you have the resolve to say something like: "Okay. It looks like we need to take a break. Let's remember that you're already getting a faster shipping time. Things are coming together for you."

Principle #5:
Take your ego out of the equation.
Let the other feel that he or she has won.

The Effective Negotiator is not looking for the "ego-win." He or she is looking to meet personal goals. The Effective Negotiator does not need to be told "you're right" or to get an apology from the other. To step out of focusing on your ego, it helps for you to review a written list of your goals multiple times during the course of the negotiation.

For example, my father would throw me against a wall when he got angry until I found a way to turn things around. When I was 15 years old and he picked me up by my hair, I coolly made a decision. I punched a hole in the wall. (Karate lessons had helped.)
He never hit me again.

I'm now in my 40's. My father has never apologized for the violence he used against me. But I still think about how my decision to punch the wall (and not my father) achieved my goal: he never hit me again.

Here is a helpful phrase: "I do not need to be proven right. I just need to gain fulfillment of my goals."

The Effective Negotiator focuses on his or her goals.

Countermeasures to 9 Dark Negotiation Methods

The Dark Negotiator has a number of favorite techniques to use against you.

Now, in the following chapters, I will discuss *Countermeasures to 9 Dark Negotiation Methods*.

We'll use the word N.E.G.O.T.I.A.T.E. to remember these methods:

N- Neutralize your power
E - Entangle you with paperwork
G - "Guilt-slam"
O - Open like a steamroller
T - Take away the goodies
I - Intimidate
A - "Anger-slap"
T - Trap
E - Encourage your fear

Let's begin with the next chapter.

Tom Marcoux

CHAPTER 2:
NEUTRALIZE YOUR POWER

The first method of N.E.G.O.T.I.A.T.E. is *Neutralize Your Power*.

The Dark Negotiator neutralizes your power by giving you the impression that you do not have power. I call this giving you a "hallucination" that you don't have power. How? They use props and settings. For example, one time I went to meet with an attorney and I was invited to wait in a conference room which was richly appointed with an expensive conference table with sixteen chairs. The room had a huge window, and I glanced at the amazing view at sixteen stories up. At the time, my entrepreneurial activates had yielded only a low cash flow. So I felt intimidated by the expensive surroundings.

So what did I do? I sat at the head of the table. Why not? I was the prospective client, bringing in the case and the opportunity for the attorney to make money. The head of the table is where the most powerful person sits, like the key partner of the law firm.

Here are three Countermeasures against someone trying to neutralize your power:

a) Take the position of power.

Above I mentioned taking the "powerseat." Here's another example: When I received my first contract from a movie distributor, I decided to take a position of power. At home, I pulled out an audio recorder and recorded 37 points that I would not agree to.

After I submitted my requested changes (by writing them on a draft of the contract) and after some discussions I gained most of the changes that I wanted.

I realized one truism. *If they are talking with me, I have more power than I might have first thought.* Why? They want something from me (the right to distribute my feature film).

b) Avoid self-critical comments.

To enhance your power in a situation, avoid words of self-criticism that lower your self-esteem. For example, Cindy undercut her own power by saying: "I'm just a teacher. What do I know about attorneys and the law?" Do not say words like this out loud. Do not undermine your credibility (in your own mind) and out loud.

c) Tell yourself empowering stories.

Before you go into a situation in which you'll be negotiating, it helps to look at a 3 x 5 card that includes notes about moments in which you were effective and courageous. You want to return yourself to an empowered state of being. When you get connected to your feelings of being strong,

22

you become more resourceful. You're able to think more clearly and recall methods that are helpful to you. Also, you have more flexibility in the moment. Even your awareness will be keener.

Point to Remember:

The Dark Negotiator tries to give you a "hallucination" that you do not have any power. Be sure to counteract this method by taking a position of power.

Your Countermeasure:

Enhance your own power by assuming a position of power and telling yourself empowering stories.

CHAPTER 3:
ENTANGLE YOU WITH PAPERWORK

Insert The second method of N.E.G.O.T.I.A.T.E. is
Entangle you with paperwork

On the first page of this book I wrote about how I felt that
someone I trusted was attempting to "force me" to settle for
an amount that was too low, considering my expenses.

To get me to agree, he wrote me a letter including these
words: "If you do not approve this settlement, this office
cannot further represent you."

Well, damn. Now, I understand that this guy has the right
to guard his own time and efforts expended. And, I'm here
to talk about how I felt being on the receiving end of his
letter.

Furthermore, he wrote in that letter that he had done "a
final round of negotiations."

Here are three Countermeasures against someone trying to entangle you with paperwork:

a) Tell yourself that what the other has written is "an opinion"

When someone writes "Final settlement" as the subject of an email or within a letter, it appears that the negotiation is over. It is not! That is, if you have not signed an agreement, the negotiation is ongoing. The words "final settlement" are the other person's opinion. Just an opinion. You can ask for "just one more round of negotiations." You can bring up a new idea and say, "I read your email. I have a new idea. Let's talk about this."

b) Give yourself "thinkspace."

You need to give yourself time and space so that you can calmly think about details. I call this "thinkspace." You can reply to the other with your own email message of "Thank you for your efforts. I will reflect on this. I'll reply to you as soon as I can."

I have met people who pride themselves on being "super-professionals." They feel it is necessary to have a fast turnaround and quickly supply people with what they requested. Instead, you are not obligated to drop everything and reply "as fast you can." You can interpret the words "as soon as I can" as the short form of "as soon I can give myself time and space to calmly think about this. I may need to sleep on it (have a good night's sleep) and get back to you tomorrow [or later]."

c) Go over the written message with someone truly on

your side.

Let's face it. Even if someone is functioning as your representative, he or she is likely to protect him or herself first. The representative may protect himself from extra work or effort. For example, your representative may have his or her assistant do much of the work. I recall getting a letter in which my representative's assistant stated that she was stuck. She was unable to get Joe, the opposing insurance company's representative, to reply to phone calls and emails. So I took action. I said, "Please give me the phone number of Joe's supervisor." I called Joe's supervisor and my message resulted in Joe sending the needed document in two days.

My point in sharing the above story is: *Do not allow a written message to stop you from considering other options.* In addition, do not allow someone else's inaction to prevent you from taking appropriate action.

Use two crucial details to ensure that you take appropriate action:

i) Talk with someone who does not have a financial stake in getting you to follow a particular course of action. I find it helpful to talk with trusted advisors and friends.

ii) Get access to your own intuition. It's vitally important to listen to yourself as you talk with your friend. You want to gain access to your own feelings and your own intuition.

Many people feel on a subconscious level that a written message has legitimacy and power. Again, I mention that a written message is somebody's opinion. You can even remind yourself by saying out loud, "That's his (her) opinion" as you read a letter or email message. Even if a written message includes the words "final settlement," you may still have important maneuvering room.

Avoid making a hasty decision. You can reply with an email message of "I'll need to reflect on this."

Point to Remember:
Realize that even though a written message seems forceful, you may still have more maneuvering room.

Your Countermeasure:
Get yourself thinkspace. Reply with a message of "I'll need to reflect on this."

CHAPTER 4:
"GUILT-SLAM"

The third method of N.E.G.O.T.I.A.T.E. is *"Guilt-slam."*

I admit it: I've created a new word, "guilt-slam." Why? Because I've seen my father use guilt thousands of times. He likes to get his way or to gain power by throwing guilt at family members.

Often, with audiences, I've said, "There are guilt-throwers and guilt-catchers. And they find each other!"

After chuckles and knowing nods of audience members, I follow up with: "Every time my father throws guilt at me, I duck!"

Here are three Countermeasures against someone trying to slam you with guilt:

a) Ask yourself: "Is this person, in this moment, on my

side?"

When someone slams you with guilt, whose side is the person on? His or her own side. Why? Because the guilt-thrower is using something that worked in the past to get personal needs fulfilled now.

On the other hand, sometimes a friend can do something positive in showing us a new perspective. Your friend could point out that you made a mistake She could even point out whose feelings were hurt. However, "rubbing it in" and trying to make you feel wrong and bad is the guilt-thrower's usual technique.

You could respond, "Thanks for telling me about that. I'll give it some good thought." In some situations, this comment may cool down the guilt-thrower a bit.

b) Connect with your own approval of some facet of yourself.

The approval you really need is your own. I have noted on my blog (BeHeardandBeTrusted.com) that "Someone's approval is like an occasional dessert. It helps to avoid 'demanding' approval. We just enjoy it when it occasionally shows up."

One way to express approval for yourself is to write down positive things in your own personal journal. I keep a personal journal entitled *Daily Journal of Victories and Blessings.*

Researchers note that it takes 10 seconds for a positive detail to impact our long-term memory. This is an important distinction. Negative feelings or impressions are instantly recorded because the amygdala (part of your brain) is on constant alert. But we must make a conscious decision to focus on something positive and have that recorded in our long-term memory. So I invite you to write for two minutes each night just before you go to sleep about the positive details that occurred during your day.

One mother I know slams her grown daughter, "Tina," by saying, "You don't visit enough." Tina reminds herself that she visits every other week and that she stays in touch by telephone. Tina reminds herself that she feels good about her consistent efforts.

c) Find compassion for yourself and the other person.

Here's a secret: the Effective Negotiator knows how to be good to him or herself—and to the other person, as appropriate. Why? This approach makes you strong and helps you make a positive connection with the other person.

For example, in recent years, I interact with a difficult member of my extended family who has become brittle and bitter. I have decided to show compassion for her and for myself. I continue to reach out to her. And I take care of myself to schedule certain days when I prefer peace and quiet (I choose to avoid calling her on those days).

If a friend or family member is in a difficult time of life, then you must take good care of yourself so that you're strong and patient. (I'm not talking about enduring abuse.) I'm talking about letting some unkind words flow past, if that is appropriate. This is a matter of "being the better person in the moment." So have compassion for the person in distress and yourself. Limit your exposure time.

The Effective Negotiator knows how to "be the better person in the moment." Why? First, it is simply a way to feel better about yourself; and you are more likely to secure cooperation if you do not lose your cool and do not escalate the bad feelings.

Point to Remember:

A guilt-thrower uses guilt against you because it has worked in the past. Avoid letting yourself get pushed around. Connect with your own approval for some facet of yourself.

Your Countermeasure:

Find compassion for yourself and the other person.

CHAPTER 5:
OPEN LIKE A STEAMROLLER

The fourth method of N.E.G.O.T.I.A.T.E. is *Open like a steamroller*.

Some people start a negotiation by making intense, unreasonable demands. Certain individuals want to unnerve the person on the other side of the table.

Here are three Countermeasures against someone trying to overwhelm you:

a) Get some thinkspace.
You can say something like, "So what I'm hearing is that part of the project is important to you. Do I have that about right?" The other says, "Yeah." You continue with: "I'll need to reflect on this. Let's keep talking."

Perhaps you might say that you need to take a restroom

break. In your own mind, you have chosen to take a break so you can get thinkspace and also break the unreasonable person's momentum.

b) Connect with what is good and strong in your life before your return to the interaction.

Some people use dark negotiation methods to send us into a downward emotional spin. They want to get us off balance. They use methods to get us hurting so we can't think straight. When we're not thinking clearly, some Dark Negotiators go in for the kill.

Your best move is to get your ego out of the equation. How? Take some time away and reconnect with the good and strong parts of your life. You could review a written list of your goals for your life. You could look at photos of loved ones or another written list of what you're grateful for in your daily life.

Then, you can review your written goals for this particular negotiation. Answer these questions: Why are you engaging in this negotiation anyway? What is to be gained?

Several years ago, I was walking with my then-girlfriend at night near Delores Park, San Francisco. I heard some noise from behind us. I glanced back and immediately pressed my girlfriend to the side—so a bicycle with two teenagers on it did not careen into her. The bicycle's handle bar hit the corner of my jacket.

The bicycle had almost hit us because the teen on the handle bars blocked the view of the other teen pedaling the bicycle.

First, I ascertained that my girlfriend was fine. I was angry that the unthinking teenagers had almost hurt my beloved. But then I reminded myself of two things:

i) There's no teaching moment here. [A teaching moment is when someone comes to you and wants instruction.]

ii) Do not engage in mischief. [Often, people have no connection or one person may be too upset. Trying to communicate at that moment may just create an argument.]

There was nothing to be gained from trying to yell and straighten out the teenagers. The teenagers were several feet away. They would not listen to any instructions from me. And a useless argument would only detract from my evening with my girlfriend.

With this story, I'm illustrating three points:

i) The teenagers came on like a streamroller. They nearly ran us over.

ii) I was angry about the possible injury to my girlfriend, but I reconnected with my true goal quickly. What goal? The plan was for my girlfriend and I to have an enjoyable evening.

iii) I'm encouraging you to reconnect with your goals for the negotiation.

And more than that, I want you to reconnect with your intrinsic value as a human being. Let's face it: people who use steamrolling techniques often think they'll win if they can back us into a corner of feeling off balance or unsure of ourselves (and our worth).

Like the teenagers, the other (who attempts to use steamrolling upon you) may be someone you need to avoid for a time (for example, by taking a short break).

During your break from the negotiation session, answer these questions for yourself:
- What am I proud of myself for?
- How do I bring a positive contribution to other people's lives?
- What is good about my life? (Consider your friends, family, talents, skills, opportunities.)

Fortify yourself before you return to the room for further negotiations.

c) Gently express to the other what you see is going on.

There's an old phrase: "He calls them as he sees them." It may be necessary for you to gently express to the other what you see is going on. Sometimes, you need to call attention to what is going on in the negotiation room. In a way, you are gently calling the other on his or her behavior.

You may want to say to the other, something like:

1) Whoa! I'm feeling like there's intense energy in the room. So let me see if I'm understanding that you want . . ."

2) "Ouch! That's a bit strong. I'm going to step over to get a cup of water and think about the details you just mentioned."

3) "Hmmm. This is more intense today. Are things going okay?"

[You're opening the door with your question to the other. Maybe the other will reply: "It's kind of tough right now. I got a call from my brother in Nebraska. My mother just went back into the hospital". . . . This is an opportunity for you and the other to make a positive connection as two people.]

Point to Remember:
Fortify yourself by reconnecting with what is good and strong in your life.

Your Countermeasure:
Get your thinkspace and reconnect with your goals and your intrinsic value as a human being.

CHAPTER 6:
TAKE AWAY THE GOODIES

The fifth method of N.E.G.O.T.I.A.T.E. is *Take away the goodies.*

One year, I met with a friend a couple of days before his birthday. I gave him the gift of a valuable book. For family reasons, I could not attend his birthday party. When I called to follow up, he said, "I'm done with the book!" My friend's pain and upset were clear. He communicated with his tone that "any good feelings about the gift do not exist. Your effort means nothing."

I call my friend's tactic "taking away the goodies." All the value was thrown away.

Here are three Countermeasures against someone trying to control you by taking away the goodies:

a) Before the negotiation, give the situation a hard look and see if you can walk away.

By walk away, I mean see if you could avoid the whole negotiation situation. Someone who consistently uses the tactic *take away the goodies* may be someone who is ultimately wasting your time. Negative people are time-drainers. When you eliminate some negative people from your work-life, you open the door to plenty of positive people to work with out there.

An old phrase goes something like this: "Money can be replaced. Time cannot be replaced."

b) Identify what is good in your life that the other person has no hold on.

This method has proven valuable to my clients who have had difficulties with older relatives. For some people, getting older is a process of watching all one's power ebb away. These older people are actually in distress. Although you acknowledge an older person's distress, you still must take care of yourself. I'm not saying that the distress excuses abuse.

Still, many people choose to do the right thing and to continue to offer assistance to elders. The solution is to fortify yourself: focus on what is good in your life that the other person has no hold on.

A bitter elder may withhold love and approval. Then, get love and approval somewhere else!

c) Devise ways you'll still live well without the goodies in the other person's control.

When we talk about goodies, we often refer to anything

that you're seeking to gain by the negotiation. The ultimate freedom is for you to be able to walk away from engaging in the negotiation at all. The other can sense if you're desperate. Often the best negotiating happens when a person is not desperate. In fact, some people hire professional negotiators because the negotiator will not be as tied to the outcome of the negotiation.

Some people think that bluffing is a good tactic to show that they are not desperate. However, many people are not good at bluffing. So I'm not here to encourage you to bluff. However, you can use these questions to strengthen yourself:

- How can I live well without what I'm negotiating for?
- What do I want? Why do I really want it?
- Can I get what I really want through another source?
- Is my ego getting in the way? Is it possible for me to walk away from this?
- Can I tone down my need? That is, can I approach this negotiation with an attitude of "oh, well, it would be nice to get what I'm aiming for, but I'd be fine without it"?

Point to Remember:
Realize that some people resort to taking away the goodies in an attempt to force you to make a quick decision. Avoid reacting. Make sure to pause and then give a measured response.

Your Countermeasure:
Find the valuable elements of your life that the other person has no hold on.

CHAPTER 7:
INTIMIDATE

The sixth method of N.E.G.O.T.I.A.T.E. is *Intimidate*.

When's the last time you felt intimidated? Was someone bigger, taller, or more commanding in tone? Did the person have special knowledge and you felt at a disadvantage?

Clients have mentioned being intimidated by gruff medical specialists like a surgeon or oncologist. Others have been intimidated by car mechanics.

Some of the tactics Dark Negotiators use include:

- They use their own language (and exclude you or leave you feeling intimidated . . . for example doctors use complicated sounding terms).
- They use a tone of voice that feels like they're putting you down.

- Some yell or even threaten physical violence.**

** *If a situation is unsafe, get professional help. Now.*

Here are three Countermeasures against someone trying to intimidate you:

a) Do your preparation work.
Be sure to keep your eyes open before you go into the negotiation. Do some reconnaissance work. For example, before I engage a new vendor I tend to use Google and type in "(Company's name) problem" and "(Company's name) scam."

Similarly, I invite you to talk with people before you go into the negotiation who have dealt with the other person you will face. Line up your methods. Prepare your "If - Then" list.

Here are some examples:
- If the other yells, then I will say, "Yelling does not work for me. I'm getting a drink of water. When I come back, if we can talk in a normal tone, we'll continue. See you in a couple of minutes."

- If the other walks out of the room in a huff, then I will send an email two days from now to see if talks can resume.

Your preparation will truly help. A number of people "fall apart" when they get startled by something extreme (like yelling or threats) and have no backup plan. But we need you to devote significant efforts to prepare. Why?

Courage is easier when you're prepared.

b) Gain real support.

It is often easier to stay strong if your own house is not divided. It is best to, as a way of life, support your family members on a regular basis: schedule time with family members as a priority just like vital business meetings. Just imagine how tough it is to be dealing with a tough negotiation at work and unrest in the home simultaneously. Avoid this double-trouble. Invest your energy and time into your loved ones. Then, they will be more likely to support you through tough times (like a tough negotiation).

Getting a coach (one to guide you through a negotiation) and rehearsing possible scenarios can really help. You'll know what to do when things get rough.

c) Do something unusual.

The person who uses intimidation is attempting to push your around. Why? Perhaps it worked on you in the past. Or at least, it has worked on others. What is the solution? Do something unusual. When the intimidator is surprised, you can swing the situation to your advantage.

One time a relative said a dark criticism to me, and I replied, "Well, that's a good one." And I chuckled. This is called a Pattern Interrupt. The conversation abruptly turned into a better direction. Why? I did not let this relative drag the conversation down into the mud.

d) End the negotiation.

Dr. Henry Cloud writes about three types of people: "wise people, foolish people, and evil people." He writes that he does not like simplistic labels, but that these categories can help a person make good choices.

For example, I was working with a video camera operator/sound recordist whom I'll call "George." After I paid him, I mentioned that the video footage of my speech had faulty audio with distracting popping sounds. I had considered George to be a friend. I said gently, "Let's talk about how we can do better next time." I included myself in the situation. Perhaps I could improve something I did, too. But he immediately got angry. At that point, he shifted to being a "foolish person" because foolish people do not listen and they fail to learn from situations. Foolish people do not build and support business relationships. Then he threatened my physical being. At that point, he shifted to being an evil person in my perception.

I made the decision to cease interacting with him. About a year later, I happened to hear that he had passed away. I received the news with sadness.

Dr. Henry Cloud writes of "necessary endings," and to this day, I feel that I had made a good choice about a necessary ending with George.

Dr. Cloud notes that with evil people one has to use definitive methods. He writes: "Many women have to get restraining orders, as they are in relationships with destructive men and their very lives are in danger. They need to create a very firm, necessary ending, with no contact and be protected by their attorneys, police, and others: ergo, lawyers, guns (police), and money."

Dr. Cloud's three-word guideline "lawyers, (police) and money" reminds us about resources we may have to protect ourselves.

e) Exert your personal power.

One thing you can do is move your body. Stand up. Or put your hands behind your head like you own the room. There is one thing you do own: your own body. Take up more space. Gesture while opening your arms; this is taking up more space.

Another way to exert your personal power is to use your voice. You don't need to yell. But you can talk louder in a firm manner. You can also bring the tone of your voice down a bit. Some leaders including President Barack Obama sound sure and powerful because they lower their tone on the last syllable of every sentence. That makes the sentence sound like a firm conviction. The opposite is a sentence that sounds like question, that is, the tone of a sentence goes up at the end.

In addition, choose your words carefully. See the big difference between:

- So, you'll support me? [Can you hear the plaintive high tone on "me"?]
- So, I'm trusting that you'll support me.

To exert your personal power is to stand your ground when you face someone using an intimidation tactic during a negotiation. Let's face it, intimidators are used to getting their way by inciting your fear. The answer is to become skillful about taming your fear. It's time to discuss one of the biggest impediments to negotiating well: Fear. I first discussed this on my blog at

www.BeHeardandBeTrusted.com

Tame the Fear; Claim Your Success

"There's so much I want to do, but I'm afraid of what could go wrong," Teresa told her personal coach, Julia. Every top successful person I've interviewed has assured me that he or she needed to feel the fear and take action, anyway. The key is to tame the fear and move forward at the same time. How do you do the extraordinary? You tame the fear.

You learn to live with the fear and get valuable support, coaching and useful feedback. Your ability to tame your own fear is essential for you to consistently get good results in negotiation.

By necessity, I've learned to feel fear and still move forward with trying new activities.

My father would never have attempted the many things I have done in the following roles:

- Feature film actor, director, producer, screenwriter
- Model for print and media (Union Bank, Peoplesoft, etc.)
- Guest instructor at Stanford University
- Author of 19 books on Amazon.com
- Lead singer/keyboard player for a band
- and more

From the age of 9 while directing my first film, I have done things that brought fear—but my healthy desire to do things overrode it.

When it comes to negotiation, many people often fail to get a fair result because their fear gets in the way. They need to learn to T.A.M.E. their fear:

T - Target your healthy desires

A - Arrange rehearsal

M - Maximize support

E - Enjoy the process

1. Target your healthy desires.

We'll focus on two types of desires: healthy and unhealthy.

Fear arises out of unhealthy desires, like the desire of wanting to feel worthy by "trying to prove yourself to be worthy." Numerous psychologists note that you cannot prove yourself worthy by merely accomplishing big things. We notice how many top actors and business people still feel unworthy. They also fear "being caught at just being lucky and not being truly talented or skillful." Related to this, a number of authors reference "the imposter syndrome," feeling like an imposter in one's own life.

Another unhealthy desire is "obsessed ambition." For example, an athlete stuck in ambition and fear can often "choke"—that is, make a big mistake when the pressure is on. Why would ambition to do this? It's not just ambition. Ambition can be a healthy part of one's life. The important word is part. The problem with obsessed ambition is that striving becomes the center and "be all" of one's life. The happiest people I know have a healthy mix of compassion, the giving of love and ambition. Their ambition is about making a contribution to the benefit of other people and expressing their personal gifts. It is not the "gimme-gimme" form of ambition. It's more about: "This is how I participate with life; this is how I make a contribution."

On the other hand, the athlete who is "in the moment" and "in the zone" will usually do well. Similarly, when you're focused on healthy desires of dedication, commitment, and love, you get "into the zone" of living full out. You then truly enjoy your life; that is, you have an energized and fulfilling stance with life (whether or not a particular situation goes as you prefer).

Some people may look upon dedication, commitment and love as character traits. Here we're referring to them in terms of the desire to engage with life in these particular ways: devoting dedication, demonstrating commitment and expressing love.

The healthy desires of dedication, commitment and love can give you the energy to work with your fear while you move forward.

Many people find it truly tough to just eliminate fear in their life.

I have observed that successful people learn to tame the fear and claim their success.

Focus on (target) your healthy desires of dedication, commitment and love.
- What do you love to do?
- What gets you excited to get up in the morning?
- What would you do even if you were not paid to do it?

Darkest Secrets of Negotiation Masters

When you start with your answers to the above questions, you can leap forward into the next chapter of your life, one filled with more success and fulfillment.

In negotiation, you need to know what you truly want. This knowledge will give you access to lots of energy for preparation. How? Imagine this: you're stuck doing the dishes and a family member says, "How about we go see that movie you really want to see?" Suddenly, you feel a surge of energy to get those dishes done quickly and get to that movie theater. Where did that energy come from? Something you really want.

2. Arrange rehearsal.
Do you fear an upcoming speech, presentation or negotiation? Here's the true solution to dealing with fear: You need to condition yourself to do what is effective. How? Rehearse! Don't have much time? How about 9 minutes a day?

Nine-minute rehearsal sessions over a sequence of days will provide you with more benefits than a single two-hour, last-minute cram session on the morning of the speech. Why? Because your subconscious mind will be working on your speech in between the daily 9 minute sessions. Some authors refer to the idea of "lateral thinking." That is, your subconscious mind keeps mulling over a problem while you're doing something else. Ever have to write a report and you get stuck? If you take a walk and get a drink of water, you're likely to have a good idea pop in your mind while you're away from your desk.

Researchers note that people, under stress, fall back on the negative default-setting behaviors. This is important to know so that you do better in a negotiation. To be at your best, you need to rehearse so that you have ingrained new patterns of behavior.

3. Maximize support.

I have experienced some fear while writing my own books. Why? Because any artist or writer gets concerned about doing a good job and not being criticized. It's only a human reaction or concern. At this point, I've written 19 books (all books on Amazon.com). Recently, someone asked, "If you felt fear, why did you write the books?" I replied, "Because I want to communicate. I want to be of service to my readers."

You see, my want is bigger than my fear. How do I do excellent work and tame my fear? I always have an excellent team to push me to better writing. I read my writing out loud to a team member and then I put the writing through two editors (I revise the work after each editor provides comments).

The solution for dealing with fear is: Maximize the support in your life. Get empowering feedback from coaches and mentors.

"Surround yourself with only people who are going to lift you higher," Oprah said. (It sure has worked for her!)

4. Enjoy the process.

Some of the best moments I have enjoyed have included an element of fear. For example, I was asked a tough question while I was addressing an audience of 600 people. For a moment, I experienced fear. Why? I didn't know how I was going to answer the particular question.

I said, "I'll need to pause for a moment. I want to make sure my answer will be valuable to you." By the time I finished saying these two sentences I had the answer in mind.

I've learned that enjoying life is not about avoiding all stress. No! We're talking about becoming strategic about the stress you let into your life.

So many times I have heard people say, "I'll do that after _____." And over the recent 11 years, I have seen certain individuals do . . . nothing!

It's sad to note that some individuals do not seem to understand that life is an "AND" process.

Focus on your healthy desires of dedication, commitment and love

AND tame your fear. Keep moving forward.

Here are examples of how life is an "AND" process:

- I'll take steps forward AND I'll feel some fear along the way.

- I'll write that novel AND I'll devote just a couple of hours to housework this week.

- I'll devote time with my family and friends AND I'll come home and write for at least 15 minutes. [I have a method I call "15, 15," that is, 15 minutes for 15 days.]

Remember:
Tame your fear and claim your success.

Don't wait to take an appropriate risk until you feel comfortable.

A bit of nervousness means you're alive! and something is important to you.

Good!

Use that nervous energy to help you get coaching, to rehearse and to be fully in the moment with your senses and sensibility functioning at their peak.

In this way, you'll enjoy peak experiences. And you become better at negotiating.

Point to Remember:
Intimidators seek to incite your fear. The solution is preparation.

Your Countermeasure:
Rehearse how you'll communicate under pressure. Consider getting a coach to guide you.

CHAPTER 8:
"ANGER-SLAP"

The seventh method of N.E.G.O.T.I.A.T.E. is *"Anger-slap"*.

I have made up a phrase, "anger-slap," to embody the sensation of how anger feels. It's like being hit.

During college I had a roommate who did a "karate chop" to my chest. It seemed that he was frustrated that I was working at the college TV studio at all hours and sleeping during the day in our dorm room. When my roommate hit my chest, it hurt but it wasn't crippling. But what hurt more was the feeling of betrayal.

After that incident, we patched up the friendship. But just remembering that moment as I type these words triggers me to slam back into the bad feelings.

When a Dark Negotiator does an "anger-slap," pay

attention. Get yourself to a safe place. And also notice if you're being triggered to re-experience painful feelings from your past. You may find working with a counselor or therapist to be truly helpful.

Here are three Countermeasures against someone trying to "anger-slap" you:

a) First, make sure that you are safe.

If someone slaps you, stop everything. Get out of there! Make sure you are safe. Even if you're verbally slapped, you can get help.

For example, one of my clients always brings a friend when she visits her parents. Why? Because her parents would gang up on her and deny that she had been sexually abused by her uncle. She also set it up that she would only visit with her parents at a local coffee shop. What reason? Her parents would be more civil in a public setting.

b) Get real support fast.

One truly insidious thing that angry people do is "make it your fault." They use lots of words like "You made me angry" or "It's your fault that I'm upset" or "Are you telling me that you didn't cause any trouble here?!"

These above statements can actually get you to doubt yourself.

Sometimes, you actually need to repeat the angry statements to a counselor or therapist who can help you discover that you were actually being manipulated to feel bad about yourself. The truth is: some people are really mentally twisted and they attempt to feel better by stepping on other people. The solution is for your to get real support fast.

If you're going into a tough negotiation, you may want to have your best friend on speed dial so you can talk with her during breaks from the negotiating session.

By the way, there is power in numbers. So if you feel it helps, you can bring in a friend to sit next to you during a negotiation.

c) Step away and inform the other person that this behavior will not be tolerated.

Step back away from the offending person. Say clearly, "This does not work for me. We're done today. I won't tolerate this behavior." If you need to re-engage with this person, bring a trusted person to support you.

Change the game. For example, one of my clients visited her parents, but was thrown out of the house at 1 AM when her mother got angry (and her father backed up her mother). So my client set up her own "new rule": she never again stayed overnight at the home of her parents.

Point to Remember:

Some people feel righteous and justified to express their anger in cruel ways. Get away from them! Or at least prepare yourself to stand your own ground.

Your Countermeasure:

Think through carefully what is likely to occur with the other person. If you know that they use anger and bad behavior, prepare in advance about how you will have support and "an escape hatch." Even sitting near the door or having a trusted friend sitting outside the room can be helpful.

CHAPTER 9:
TRAP

The eighth method of N.E.G.O.T.I.A.T.E. is *Trap*.

Let's face it: some people are smooth-talkers who demonstrate a quick wit. They can trap you. How? They use almost a magic sleight of hand method of using logic. It can be along the pattern of "If you say X then Y must be included."

You do NOT have to accept the premise that the other person is proposing.

You can smile and say, "Wow. I'm surprised that you'd imagine that idea. I see it differently."

Here are three Countermeasures against someone trying to trap you:

a) Do not accept the premise that the other person tries

to use on you.

Someone who attempts to manipulate you may say something with a premise that is unfair or that tries to paint you into a corner. Just because someone expressed an opinion does not mean that opinion is true. Here is an example of a positive response: "That's an unusual opinion. I do not agree. I start from the idea of a benefit for my audience and then I build . . ."

Another way to deal with someone's unfair premise is to say something neutral like: "George, I can see that is important to you. What I can say is . . ."

The beauty of the above statement is that you're not agreeing with George. When you use the statement "What I can say is . . .", you give yourself the latitude to say what is positive for yourself.

b) Write up two lists with the titles: "10 Questions I Don't Want to Answer" and "20 Answers."

When you write up two lists "10 Questions I Don't Want to Answer" and "20 Answers," you become especially prepared. I use the title "10 Questions I Don't Want to Answer" to be an effective cue for you to write down truly tough questions.

Then, the idea is for you to come up with two answers for each of the ten questions. Remember my phrase that I mentioned earlier: "Courage is easier when you're prepared."

You'll be ready for a trap when you know how you'll respond to tough questions.

c) If you don't feel quick-witted, get someone you know who is sharp to walk through all of the possible scenarios with you.

This is another situation in which preparation is key. Get help and support. As I mentioned earlier, for every book I write, I have two editors. Having two highly intelligent people show me places where I can improve helps me to raise the level of my writing.

Point to Remember:

Some people seek to control others by trapping them or even making them look bad. Do not play their game by accepting their troublesome premise.

Your Countermeasure:

Do your homework and prepare two lists: *10 Question I Don't Want to Answer and 20 Answers.*

CHAPTER 10:
ENCOURAGE YOUR FEAR

The final method of N.E.G.O.T.I.A.T.E. is *Encourage Your Fear.*

Why does a Dark Negotiator try to get you into feeling fear? Because it works. When we're in a fearful state of being, it gives us tunnel vision. Limited vision is a major liability for a negotiator.

On the other hand, the Effective Negotiator sees "the whole chessboard," that is, he or she looks at the whole picture. When you're aware of the many variables, you can form many options for your own well being. Effective Negotiators maintain a calm, resourceful state of being.

It's hard to remain in a calm state because a Dark Negotiator will often tell you a story to get you afraid of a possible loss; this person is trying to use your emotional brain against you. The Dark Negotiator is accessing the conditioning of your brain. The part of your emotional brain called the amygdala is continually on the lookout: "Watch out, you might lose something here!" The amygdala is programmed from birth to be focused on preventing the pain of loss. Researchers note that the amygdala tends to be two times larger in a man than a woman.

The use of "scary stories" is so prevalent that you need to use countermeasures to protect yourself.

Here are three Countermeasures against someone trying to incite fear in you:

a) Face the fear.
Face the fear before the negotiation. First, assess how you will be "okay" even if the deal does not occur. It you want a deal too desperately, you may "give away the store." It is reported that some negotiators use an insidious tactic when an American visits their country. They find out when an American negotiator will be flying home. Then the negotiators do all kinds of delaying tactics (often involving nightclubs and drinking). Finally, when the American is leaving the country, he or she is trying to negotiate in the car on the way to the airport. Why is this effective? Because the American is terrified to return home with no deal.

Don't let yourself get manipulated. Identify your fears before the negotiation and write up your personal strategy and plan. Have a plan to deal with delaying tactics. For example, do not disclose your actual departure date from the country. You could say, "We'll see how this goes. I have some flexibility here."

b) Admit the fear (after you're outside the room and talking with someone you trust).

As soon as you voice your fear to a trusted friend or family member, you decrease the power. How? The hidden fear gives one general jitters, and it's often referred to as free-floating anxiety. Now that you have voiced the fear, you can build your strategies to counteract the bad outcomes you want to avoid. The act of thinking of solutions lessens anxiety. Just shining the light on the fear often makes it feel smaller.

Ask yourself before the negotiation (and at intervals during the negotiation):

- What's the worst that can happen?
- How can I reduce the likelihood of that happening?
- If it did happen, how can I reduce the damage?
- Who can help me?
- How can I help myself to live well even if this thing I fear took place?

c) Uncover how you can live with the feared thing occurring.

I want to emphasize this step because I have personally been amazed at how people can live with tough things. I know people who have medical difficulties and they're living from one test to the next. But the good news is that they do not focus on fear throughout the day. In fact, a number of survivors of serious illness talk about how facing mortality has intensified their appreciation of each day and each moment. Many of these survivors suddenly went into high gear to shake off their fears and try new adventures in life.

Point to Remember:
Induced fear can bring tunnel vision. It is important to face the fear and discuss it with a trusted friend, counselor or therapist. You then reduce fear's power.

Your Countermeasure:
Discuss your fear with a trusted friend, counselor or therapist. Then identify ways you can reduce the likelihood of the feared thing occurring.

CONCLUSION TO BOOK I: DARKEST SECRETS OF NEGOTIATION MASTERS

In this section we have learned 9 Dark Negotiation Methods that include:

N- Neutralize your power
E - Entangle you with paperwork
G - "Guilt-slam"
O - Open like a steamroller
T - Take away the goodies
I - Intimidate
A - "Anger-slap"
T - Trap
E - Encourage your fear

And you learned countermeasures to the above dark methods.

In *Book II*, we'll discuss methods to *Turn Effective*

Negotiating Power to Good.
   Let's move forward . . .

.

BOOK II
TURN EFFECTIVE NEGOTIATING POWER
TO GOOD—INTRODUCTION

To be an Effective Negotiator, you need good access to your intuition.

Why is your intuition so important? Researchers note that intuition is the part of a human being that has access to knowledge not in the conscious, rational mind. That means that the person who is intuitive often has an advantage over someone who "simply lives in his head."

Using your intuition is a special advantage in negotiation. Donald Trump is noted for his deal-making skills and he said, "Experience taught me a few things. One is to listen to your gut, no matter how good something sounds on paper."

Oprah Winfrey said, "Learn to let your intuition—gut instinct—tell you when the food, the relationship, the job isn't good for you (and conversely, when what you're doing is just right)."

It helps to use all your resources, including intuition, for effective negotiating and decision-making.

The heart has its reasons of which reason knows nothing.
— Blaise Pascal

Research scientist Gerd Gigerenzer, in his book *Gut Feelings: The Intelligence of the Unconscious*, wrote about how his friend "Harry" was confronted with a choice between two young women. Harry wanted to exclusively date only one of these women. So, he wrote down his reasons about whether to choose one or the other woman in a logical fashion.

As Gerd Gigerenzer wrote: "Harry was greatly relieved that a logical formula existed to solve his conflict. So he took his time, wrote down all the important reasons he could think of, weighed them carefully, and went through the calculation. When he saw the result, something unexpected happened. An inner voice told him that it wasn't right.

And for the first time, Harry realized that his heart had already decided—against the calculation and in favor of the other girl. The calculus helped to find the solution, but not because of its logic. It brought an unconscious decision to his awareness, based on reasons obscure to him."

Gerd Gigerenzer was making a point about "unconscious intelligence." That is, we have a source of effective decision-making that is beyond the level of conscious thought.

I have also found that using a Pro vs. Con List to be

helpful in making good decisions. Several years ago, I had the opportunity to take a full-time job in a major corporation. I quickly wrote down nine reasons to take the job, including good compensation and good location. Then I wrote a list of reasons against taking the job. When I wrote the third Con detail, it practically leapt off the page. It was about the management style of the leadership of the department. This one reason was more important to me than nine reasons to take the job. Years later, my sweetheart described what she feels happened: "The one Con reason was like a watermelon and the nine Pro reasons were just peas."

I'm so glad that I had gained access to my intuition through the use of a Pro vs. Con List.

Intuition is one of our most important strengths for negotiating well. Let's explore the I.N.T.U.I.T. process:

I - Identify the Crucial Detail
N - Name who you report to
T - Talk about how it's okay for you to be brief
U - Understand "LAR" and "MSP"
I - Invite connection
T - Tell a story

CHAPTER 11:
IDENTIFY THE CRUCIAL DETAIL

If you don't know what you deeply and truly want, you are vulnerable to manipulation. You need to identify the Crucial Detail. How? Often you need to "stumble upon it." I have found it useful to talk with a trusted friend or advisor. As I'm talking, I discover how I really feel about some detail. While I'm talking, I'm getting access to my feelings and intuition. This is a useful process.

Often, we can be mistaken as to what is the true Crucial Detail. Why? The first of two reasons is that we're not connected to our intuition or our heart. The second reason is that our ego may block our sight or hearing.

Here's an example about hearing that I often label: "Friendship made me deaf." Some years ago, I was producing a song for a motion picture that I was directing. In the recording studio, I was listening to my friend as he sang during the choruses of the song. Because of our friendship, I wanted him to sound good. But this was not the Crucial Detail.

In essence, my focus on my friend made me "temporarily deaf." The song ended up with the lead vocalist singing too low in her vocal range. So my friend sounded good, the lead vocalist sounded bad, and I could not use the song in the feature film. What a waste of time and money. What was the Crucial Detail here? It was how the lead vocalist sounded.

Again, I encourage your to talk with trusted friends and advisors and listen to what you say and uncover what your heart is saying.

Point to Remember:
Be careful to look for the Crucial Detail. Realize that you need to look deep because you could be distracted by the ego or something else.

Your Action Step:
Devote time to talking with trusted friends and advisors and listen to what you say and uncover what your heart is saying.

CHAPTER 12:
NAME WHO YOU REPORT TO

To get access to your intuition, you need time and space to think and feel. Often in this book, I refer to getting "thinkspace." One powerful way to do this is to mention that you need to talk with an advisor. You could say, "I'll need to talk this over with my [lawyer, accountant, spouse, team members, marketing coach, board of directors, etc.]."

Why do you want to mention who you "report to"? Because a salesperson wants to pin you down and find out that you're the final decision-maker. If you're that person, the salesperson wants to push you to make a decision now.

Even if you are the final decision maker, do not reveal that detail. A smooth negotiator will try to get you to agree and commit to something, perhaps, without you having appropriate thinkspace to get access to your intuition.

Warning: if something feels off, listen to it! That's most likely your intuition vying for your attention. I have heard many people say that they got in the most trouble when they did not listen to an intuitive feeling.

If there is no urgent deadline, I will actually schedule getting a good night's sleep before I make a vital commitment of time, money and resources to a project. How does this relate to negotiating? Tired people give in too easily in a negotiation. On a feeling level, a tired person just want the negotiations to end. Don't let personal fatigue push you into making bad decisions and bad deals.

Point to Remember:
You need thinkspace, so identify that you "report to someone."

Your Action Step:
Prepare by choosing which person or group you will say is someone you "report to."

CHAPTER 13: TALK ABOUT HOW IT'S OKAY FOR YOU TO BE BRIEF

A number of people use this preamble: "To be honest with you . . ." This is a mistake. Why? It turns a bad light upon everything else a person has said. It implies that he or she was not honest before, and this person may not be honest in the future.

Instead, I give myself permission to state things in a to-the-point manner. I use a preamble like: "To put it in a few words" or "To be concise." By using this phrase, you can basically set the stage that it is okay for you to be brief and to the point.

It can be helpful to be brief and to the point. How? You might say something that is intuitive. You might discover your true feelings.

Point to Remember:
Avoid saying "To be honest with you . . ."

Your Action Step:
Consider saying "to put it in a few words" or "to be concise."

.

CHAPTER 14:
UNDERSTAND "LAR" AND "MSP"

Author Herb Cohen wrote about two vital concepts for effective negotiating: Least Acceptable Result (LAR) and Maximum Supportable Position (MSP).

The LAR is the minimum of what would be okay for you. For example, if you were selling your used car, you might ask for $6,000, but you might settle for $3,990. If the other person offers $4,030, you could decide to say yes because you're still doing better than $3,990.

The MSP is a high goal but one that is supportable by corroborating facts. For example, a personal coach who has been working for two years might state that she works at $400 per hour. That's high, but it may be backed up by credible testimonials about her effectiveness and how her clients have excelled. On the other hand, a number of people would find a proposed fee of $30,000 per hour to be unlikely.

My innovation is to give you questions for determining your LAR and MSP to help you gain access to your intuitive responses.

For Least Acceptable Result (LAR):
- What could I put up with?

For Maximum Supportable Position (MSP):
- If the Genie from Aladdin were here, what would I ask for?

Your first answer to the MSP question can give you insight as to what you want on an intuitive level. The next step is to marshal your supporting evidence so that your MSP is not an outlandish request. For example, you can gather testimonials that prove the efficacy of your service or product.

Point to Remember:
Use tools like LAR and MSP to help you gain access to your intuitive answers.

Your Action Step:
Answer the two questions of LAR and MSP and write down your first responses.

CHAPTER 15:
INVITE CONNECTION

Imagine that we're sitting in a helicopter above the negotiation that you're dealing with. Now, as we have a view of the two (or more) people involved, what do you feel is really going on here?

Both people have these thoughts:

- Can I get what I want?
- Can I trust the other person?

Subconscious thoughts/questions are going on, too:

- Am I worthy of getting exactly what I want?
- Will this person hurt me?
- Is this person like someone who hurt me in the past?

Let's pause for a moment and think about this question: What is going to make good things happen in this negotiation? The answer is you need to develop your prime skills of making a good connection with the other person.

When you're listening, you're winning.

Why? You're guiding the person to become receptive to something you subsequently say. How does this work? When two people meet there is an immediate tension. Each person is trying to express their thoughts and feelings. When you listen first, you create some level of comfort in the other person. In essence, you are disarming the person.

Currently, my book *Be Heard and Be Trusted* is in its Third Edition. In fact, a copy of the first edition is in the Cogswell Polytechnical College Time Capsule to be opened in the year 2100. How could something written in 2000 be of use 100 years later? The book talks about how to listen and how to express oneself in a trust-inducing manner. These are timeless topics.

I mentioned this earlier, but this information is so important, I'll repeat it here. Here are actions that I call the *3 Listening Blockers*.

1) Judging
We judge things all of the time. "Yes, she's right." "No, he's wrong." The solution is to put our judgment on hold in our mind, and ask a gentle follow-up question. You could ask something like: "It sounds like Section 7 is important to you. Is that about right?"

2) Defending
People say, "No! I don't always forget to take out the garbage. I took it out last week!" Instead of cutting off the other person, it helps to ask a couple of questions to help the person complete expressing her feelings. It takes practice to ask, "Is there anything else?" You might wonder why you

would ask such a question. What you're doing is creating the space for the other person to express themselves more fully. Eventually, the person will experience some form of ease because at last he or she has been heard.

3) Me, too—One Up

Sometimes, we might say something like, "Yes. I can understand. I have three children [when the person was complaining about his one child]." At first glance, it seems like we're sympathizing or even empathizing with the person's situation. But when we "one up," we're turning the spotlight (of the conversation) back upon ourselves. The person is now metaphorically in the dark, and he or she does not like that! When you catch yourself doing "me, too—one up," pause and ask a gentle question. Here's an example of a gentle question: "That sounds like a tough situation. So how did you feel about ___?"

Remember, when you ask a gentle question, you turn that conversation spotlight back upon the other person.

What is the solution to the tendency to do "me, too—one up"? Observe your own behavior during a conversation. When you fall into a listening blocker-behavior, turn your attention to the other person and ask a gentle question. For example, you could say:

a) That sounds like it was frustrating. What did you hope would happen?

b) That sounds like it felt overwhelming. What is your plan?

You might wonder what makes the above "gentle questions." First, you acknowledge that the person may be feeling some painful emotion. Notice, you do not categorically say that the person was definitely feeling a particular emotion. You qualify your comment with "that sounds like." Second, you ask for more input from the person. You give him or her the chance to express more feelings. You create the space for the person to feel heard. Effective Negotiators are good listeners. It takes practice.

Point to Remember:

Being an Effective Negotiator means that you have developed your prime skills of making a good connection with the other person.

Your Action Step:

Practice observing your own behavior. Have you noticed that you tend to fall into one of the *3 Listening Blockers?* If so, practice asking a gentle question to turn the spotlight back upon the other person.

CHAPTER 16:
TELL A STORY

One of my clients was confronted with a letter from her attorney that stated that the health maintenance organization representative said additional medical charges were not included in the total bill. The attorney assured her that that was just a verbal mistake.

My client wrote to her attorney: "I cannot agree to this settlement situation. Here is information to help you understand my viewpoint. I have been hit by three vehicles in my life and I have been beaten. I know bad things happen. I need to see the actual document that is signed by the HMO representative that states that $2745 is 'payment in full.'"

Do you think that her attorney sent my client the HMO representative's document "that states that $2745 is 'payment in full.'"?

Her attorney sent the document immediately. This was a good result because my client wanted documentation in case anything might be disputed in the future.

What happened here? My client told a true story that could help her attorney understand the basis for my client's need for proceeding carefully and for requiring documentation to be sent so she could have it for her own files.

In Effective Negotiating, telling a powerful story often gains good results. Why? A good story gives the other person an experience. It also avoids creating resistance. How does that work? Often, when you tell a story you can paint a picture of the personal benefit for the other person.

Here are elements of a powerful story:

1. You are a major person in the story.
2. The problem is presented, and it's a tough one.
3. There's a time crunch involved (like a "ticking time bomb").
4. It seems that there is no solution. (This provides suspense and tension.)
5. There is a surprising resolution. (This provides feelings of relief and joy.)

It may not be possible to include all five elements, but it helps to incorporate as many of the elements as possible.

Again, telling a story gives you a special advantage: Often you can avoid generating resistance in the other person. How? We are conditioned from childhood to pay attention to stories, and they give us an experience.

On the other hand, if you make a simple statement, the person automatically goes into "judging mode." The person asks him or herself, "Is that true? Do I believe that?"

Here is a technique I teach my graduate students in my public speaking class: "Don't just state a fact. At least, ask a question."

Asking a question creates a different energy in the room. Just imagine the different audience responses to a statement versus a question:

1) Women live longer than men.
2) Why do women live longer than men?

In addition, statistics can be dry. Instead, telling a story does engage the audience. I'll now share examples of two of my own stories. (I'll present the first couple of sentences of each story.)

- "When I was holding onto the hood of the Classic 50's truck going 60 miles an hour, my finger tips were aching. I wasn't thinking of the cameraman trying to get the shot. I was focused on . . ."

- "When I held the hand of my mother who was awake and undergoing a breast lumpectomy under local anesthesia, I saw in her eyes that the pain . . ."

As you can see, the story puts you into the moment. So I invite you to hone your skills as an Effective Negotiator.

Identify your stories and rehearse them before you get to the negotiation table.

Point to Remember:
Tell a story to avoid resistance in the other person.

Your Action Step:
Craft your personal story to have a problem, suspense, tension, and a relief-giving resolution.

* * *

Now that I have shared with you the efficacy of telling stories, I'll take our discussion a step further. Often, when we hear an example or story, our intuition kicks in and we feel: "Hey, I think that would work for me, too." Similarly, many of us have heard how notable people have accomplished something, and we notice that we might be able to apply their methods to our own endeavors. Now, we'll learn the thoughts and methods of 11 millionaires and billionaires . . .

How Eleven Millionaires and Billionaires Negotiate with Others

This book is about turning the power to good. Positive persuasion methods of ten billionaires and millionaires are described below.

1. Bill Gates
Bill Gates has talked about being flexible and adaptable to changes that are rapidly occurring. He said, "People always

fear change. People feared electricity when it was invented, didn't they? People feared coal, they feared gas-powered engines... There will always be ignorance, and ignorance leads to fear." And, "Success is a lousy teacher. It seduces smart people into thinking they can't lose." He also noted, "This is a fantastic time to be entering the business world, because business is going to change more in the next 10 years than it has in the last 50." Finally, "Whether it's Google or Apple or free software, we've got some fantastic competitors and it keeps us on our toes."

2. Oprah Winfrey

Oprah has made many multi-million dollar decisions. She said, "Think like a queen. A queen is not afraid to fail. Failure is another steppingstone to greatness . . . . Turn your wounds into wisdom." And, "Before you agree to do anything that might add even the smallest amount of stress to your life, ask yourself: What is my truest intention? Give yourself time to let a yes resound within you. When it's right, I guarantee that your entire body will feel it." Also, "Be thankful for what you have; you'll end up having more. If you concentrate on what you don't have, you will never, ever have enough." She emphasizes, "Challenges are gifts that force us to search for a new center of gravity. Don't fight them. Just find a different way to stand." And, "Doing the best at this moment puts you in the best place for the next moment." She talks about choosing empowering thoughts: "Every time you state what you want or believe, you're the first to hear it. It's a message to both you and others about what you think is possible. Don't put a ceiling on yourself . . . . Follow your instincts. That's where true wisdom manifests itself." Finally, "Surround yourself with only people who are going to lift you higher."

3. Jack Canfield

(co-creator of the *Chicken Soup for the Soul* series of books and numerous products)

Jack Canfield provides audiences with hope. He wrote, "Why are people afraid to ask? They are afraid of many things such as looking needy, looking foolish, and looking stupid. But mostly they're afraid of experiencing rejection. They are afraid of hearing the word no. The sad thing is that they're actually rejecting themselves in advance. . . . Here are some quick tips: 1) Ask as if you expect to get it, 2) Assume you can, 3) Ask someone who can give it to you, 4) Be clear and specific, and 5) Ask repeatedly." He points out that one can ask multiple times:

"On a different day
When the person is in a better mood
When you have new data to present
After you've proven your commitment to them
When the circumstance have changed
When you've learned how to close better
When you've established better rapport
When the person trusts you more
When you have paid your dues
When the economy is better"

4. Mark Victor Hansen

(co-creator of the *Chicken Soup for the Soul* series of books and numerous products)

Mark Victor Hansen talks a lot about getting clear in yourself about your worth and what you want. For him, that is the starting point. He said, "You control your future, your destiny. What you think about comes about. By recording your dreams and goals on paper, you set in motion the process of becoming the person you most want to be. Put your future in good hands—your own." And, "When your self-worth goes up, your net worth goes up with it." Also, "Dedicate yourself to the good you deserve and desire for yourself. Give yourself peace of mind. You deserve to be happy. You deserve delight." He emphasizes, "Big goals get big results. No goals get no results or somebody else's results." He concludes, "Don't wait until everything is just right. It will never be perfect. There will always be challenges, obstacles and less than perfect conditions. So what. Get started now. With each step you take, you will grow stronger and stronger, more and more skilled, more and more self-confident and more and more successful."

5. Brian Tracy

Brian Tracy presents precise methods that are expressed simply and clearly. He wrote: "If you look the part, you have passed the first test of credibility. But if you look good but are apparently unprepared or confused, your newfound credibility will disappear. Prepare thoroughly for every important meeting with others, especially in business. Do your homework before every meeting." Certainly, you need to be prepared before you negotiate with anyone. He also wrote, "The purpose of a negotiation is to enter into an agreement such that both parties have their needs satisfied and are motivated to fulfill their commitments and enter into further negotiations with the same party in the future." And, he emphasizes, "[Ensure that] both parties are satisfied enough with the outcome that they are motivated to fulfill whatever commitments they have made, and they feel positively enough about the deal that they are willing to negotiate again and enter into subsequent agreements in the future."

6. Anthony Robbins

Anthony Robbins, in his presentations, energizes the listener. He said, "The single most powerful tool for winning a negotiation is the ability to get up and walk away from the table without a deal." He also points out the starting point for success: "In life you need either inspiration or desperation." Also, "I've come to believe that all my past failure and frustration were actually laying the foundation for the understandings that have created the new level of living I now enjoy." He emphasizes action and commitment: "In essence, if we want to direct our lives, we must take control of our consistent actions. It's not what we do once in a while that shapes our lives, but what we do consistently." And, "The path to success is to take massive, determined action." Also, "I believe life is constantly testing us for our level of commitment, and life's greatest rewards are reserved for those who demonstrate a never-ending commitment to act until they achieve. This level of resolve can move mountains, but it must be constant and consistent. As simplistic as this may sound, it is still the common denominator separating those who live their dreams from those who live in regret." In preparation for negotiating and during a negotiation good questions are vital. He said, "Quality questions create a quality life. Successful people ask better questions, and as a result, they get better answers." Finally, "Focus on where you want to go, not on what you fear."

7. Warren Buffet

(legendary investor and the third wealthiest person in the world)

Warren Buffet is known for his plain speech. His

approach is to take the long view. He said, "It takes 20 years to build a reputation and five minutes to ruin it. If you think about that, you'll do things differently." And, "Only buy something that you'd be perfectly happy to hold if the market shut down for 10 years." Also, "Should you find yourself in a chronically leaking boat, energy devoted to changing vessels is likely to be more productive than energy devoted to patching leaks." He noted, "Someone's sitting in the shade today because someone planted a tree a long time ago." Finally, "Your premium brand had better be delivering something special, or it's not going to get the business."

8. Donald Trump

Donald Trump is known as a go-getter who speaks bluntly. Trump's bluntness and bravado gain attention. He said, "My style of deal making is quite simple and straightforward. We just keep pushing and pushing to get what I'm after." And, "For entrepreneurs, ignorance is not bliss. It's fatal. It's costly. And it's for losers. You either get organized, or get crushed." Also, "You can't be scared. You do your thing, you hold your ground, you stand up tall, and whatever happens, happens." He emphasized, "The most important thing in life is to love what you're doing, because that's the only way you'll ever be really good at it." And, "Without passion, you don't have energy, without energy you have nothing." Also, "Watch, listen, and learn. You can't know it all yourself. Anyone who thinks they do is destined for mediocrity." And he seems to sum up his philosophy about self promotion: "If you don't tell people about your success, they probably won't know about it."

9. Suze Orman

(#1 New York Times best-selling author, known as

"America's most trusted personal finance expert")

Suze Orman is known for her straight-to-the-point comments: "You must negotiate for yourself the best interest rates, even if it means switching credit cards every six months. . . . You must understand everything about how your credit card works—all fees, how the company charges you, all about the so-called grace period, everything." And, "A big part of financial freedom is having your heart and mind free from worry about the what-ifs of life." Also, "In all realms of life it takes courage to stretch your limits, express your power, and fulfill your potential... it's no different in the financial realm." She also recommends preparation: "If you're negotiating a salary for a new job, don't wait for the offer to form your strategy. Go out and research what the going rate is for your field and for someone with your experience. Websites like Salary.com make it easy to get good salary info."

10. Richard Branson
(Founder and President of Virgin Atlantic)

A number of entrepreneurs mention that one needs the ability to walk away from a bad deal. Richard said, "Business opportunities are like buses, there's always another one coming." And, "I never get the accountants in before I start up a business. It's done on gut feeling . . . . You never know with these things when you're trying something new what can happen. This is all experimental." He noted, "We've always had a pretty competitive and pretty ferocious battle with British Airways... It's lasted now about 14 years, and we're very pleased to have survived it." In fact, British Airways' campaign against Virgin included poaching Virgin Atlantic customers and tampering with Virgin's private files. Richard Branson took his negotiation to the level of suing

British Airways. The court case ended with British Airways forced to pay Virgin Atlantic damages and legal costs.

11. Walt Disney

In 1928, Walt Disney lost the rights to his first major animated character, Oswald the Lucky Rabbit, when the shady distributor took the character and enticed many key animators away from the Disney Studio. In response, Walt said, "I will never work for someone else again." He eventually started his own distribution company Buena Vista Pictures Distribution, Inc. This gave him more options than film producers dependent on outside distributors. In 1995, the Walt Disney Company increased their distribution capabilities by purchasing Cap Cities/ABC, which had (at the time) 225 affiliate TV stations and the nation's largest radio network with 21 stations. Walt Disney said, "All the adversity I've had in my life, all my troubles and obstacles, have strengthened me... You may not realize it when it happens, but a kick in the teeth may be the best thing in the world for you."

From many of these effective people, we learn that speaking in a forthright manner gains attention, and that to succeed and negotiate on a top level, preparation is key.

CONCLUSION TO BOOK II: TURN EFFECTIVE NEGOTIATING POWER TO GOOD

In BOOK II we covered 6 Methods of Accessing Your Intuition related to Effective Negotiating:

I - Identify the Crucial Detail

N - Name who you report to

T - Talk about how it's okay for you to be brief

U - Understand "LAR" and "MSP"

I - Invite connection

T - Tell a story

We also covered the thoughts and methods of 11 millionaires and billionaires.

In *BOOK III: 10 General Principles of Effective Negotiating,* we will discuss some surprising and useful ways of approaching your next negotiation.

Let's step forward . . .

BOOK III:
10 GENERAL PRINCIPLES OF
EFFECTIVE NEGOTIATING
—CHAPTER 17

1. Make it a game you can win.

"It's not a game," my father has often said; and so, he's not good at negotiation. You need to step out of your emotional brain's tendency to make the negotiation a "life or death struggle." A powerful method is to quickly change your perspective. Just imagine that you're standing at the window, six stories above a mall area. You literally have a bird's eye view. You are also above the fray so your emotions can be quieter. When your ego and emotions are quiet, you can think clearer, see more and make better decisions than someone who is distraught. Over the years, I've learned: When you can quiet your ego and look upon negotiation as a game, you can take a higher level perspective and take good steps for what you want.

When I say "make it a game," I think about how many of

us approach a game. We take the time to learn the rules. We practice. Those of us who want to get better, at tennis for example, engage a coach.

Even if I say, "make it a game," I still affirm that it can be a serious game. If you're negotiating for a salary increase, that is serious. By the way, here is a quiet way to inquire about a raise: you could say to your supervisor, "I'm wondering about the process to earn a raise."

For many of us, pre-planning how you will ask for a raise makes sense. In addition, part of making it a game is to pre-plan how you will be okay even if the negotiation does not result in what you prefer.

Another detail about "make it a game" is that, in a game, you clearly know your goal. Again, I suggest that you put your ego aside and focus on the most important thing you want. Why? Because a skilled player will eliminate distractions. Let's face it. In a negotiation, our true focus is not about getting ego-benefits (like approval). Our true focus is getting the deeply desired benefit/result (for example, a highly functional car for a good price).

Now, let's go deeper about the "make it a game you can win" process. I've noticed that some people get themselves into situations in which they cannot win. This gave rise to my phrase: "Make it a game you can win." If you have a bitter, older relative, you might find that "getting Aunt Gertrude to be nice" or "getting Aunt Gertrude to like me" are implausible goals. A better goal may be "hold my own calm while interacting with Aunt Gertrude."

Point to Remember:
When you can quiet your ego and look upon negotiation as a game, you can take a higher level perspective and take effective action for what you want.

Your Action Step:
Use the metaphor "make it a game you can win" before and during a negotiation. Identify goals that you have a plausible chance of achieving.

2) BE OKAY THAT SOMETIMES YOU WIN, SOMETIMES YOU DON'T

In 1989, while watching the movie *Indiana Jones and The Last Crusade*, I saw the young Indiana Jones lose an antique cross to a money-grubbing adventurer. The adventurer said, while he held the prized artifact, "You lost today, kid. But that doesn't mean you have to like it."

Well, I didn't like hearing that line, and I did *not* like watching Indiana Jones lose. But after several years in business and many negotiation situations, I have learned that sometimes you win, sometimes you lose, and sometimes you come out somewhere in between.

This builds on Principle #1, "Make it a game you can win." If it is a game, then you will be using your skills and sometimes the dice do not roll your way. The empowering word is "Next!" We use that word in statements like:

- Next deal
- Next time
- Next negotiation

- Next opportunity
- Next prospective client
- Next time, one month from now, I'll approach this prospective client in a new way

When you say, "Next!" add this idea: "I'll learn what I can here and apply it to my NEXT business endeavor."

Point to Remember:
Sometimes you win, sometimes you don't. But you can get better by making sure you learn something for next time.

Your Action Step:
For each negotiation, consider making an entry in a log. Identify your answers to these questions (and you'll ensure that you learn something):
a) What did I do right?
b) What areas can I improve?
c) What opportunity did I leave on the table?
d) What type of coaching will help me be more effective next time?
e) What will I do differently next time?
f) Did something happen that was truly out of my hands?

3) REMEMBER: "IT'S ALL GOOD PRACTICE"

One year, a family member bought a ring at a jewelry store in San Francisco. The ring had a stamp that stated Sterling silver but the ring turned her finger green. I asked my family member: "What do you want?" She said that she wanted the money back. One problematic detail: the receipt said "No refunds."

Please note: this is just the start of the negotiation. So I went into the store and talked with the onsite manager who said he could not fix the situation. I asked to speak to someone with more authority. Then it became two against one (me): the onsite manager and the regional supervisor (on the phone). Here are methods that I used (not in this exact order):

Method #1: Separate the others

Let's face it. If you feel ganged up on, you'll feel more distress. See if you can somehow separate the two people (for example). Then you can focus on just one person. So I encouraged the onsite manager to end the phone call with the regional supervisor. Then I could deal one-to-one with the onsite manager.

Method #2: Use a camera

I took photos of the ring, the store, the display area and any relevant signs. I was thinking about how this showed my thoroughness.

Here's another example: several years ago, I was sitting in the backseat of a car driven by my friend. When an accident occurred, I was glad that I had a camera with me. I took photos of the people involved, the license plates and the damage to the vehicles.

Method #3: Do something unusual

I talked loudly about how the store was cheating my family member so that other customers could hear it.

Method #4: Use an incentive

I said, "Let's make this work and I'll never see you again

and you'll never see me again." The incentive was that the manager's problem would go away.

Method #5: Change your direction

So the manager said that he couldn't refund the money. So I went back to my family member and said, "How about we get you something of more value? Look at everything in the store. But do not choose another ring, please." My plan was to get something of greater value.

Method #6: Ask for too much

The receipt for the faulty jewelry read "No refunds." I took this to mean that a trade of products would be likely. However, to put it frankly, the faulty jewelry was a piece of junk. A trade for another piece of junk was not acceptable. So I brought up two of the most expensive items in the store. I knew that the manager would not agree to providing two items. The onsite manager's face looked like he felt satisfied in telling me, "No. I can't do that." I had not revealed my true goal of getting one item of greater value for my family member.

Method #7: Calculate the value—not just as money but as your time and life energy

I did not let the manager know that I was approaching the moment when I would just write off the whole situation. Here's an important detail: while I was negotiating with the unhelpful manager, I had the time of four people who are important to me to consider: my family member, two friends and myself. My two friends and family member were waiting in the costume jewelry store.

I invite you to: *Calculate the value—not just as money but as your time and life energy.*

Remember, you will not always win. Do not let a negotiation be overrun by your ego wanting to win at all costs. It's not worth it.

The outcome: my family member received something at a retail value of twice the ring. She was happy about the outcome. That was my first goal. In addition, I had this principle in mind: *It's all good practice.*

Then I said to my family member: "How about you avoid buying costume jewelry ever again?" I remembered one of my martial arts mentors said, "The best defense is not to be there."

Point to Remember:
Remember that the more you practice, the more easily you flow with the process of negotiating.

Your Action Step:
Practice your negotiation skills on transactions that are relatively minor.

4) GO AHEAD, BE UNUSUAL

One of my clients asked her representative, "Have you ever gained a better result by going to the supervisor on the other side?" Her representative replied, "That has only happened once in 29 years."

My client replied: "Good. Let's see if this will be the second time."

My client's response is an example of doing something

unusual.

Doing something unusual can be a prime negotiation tactic, particularly when you're dealing with a clerk who is quoting policy. The solution to the blockage made by the clerk and policy is for you to go up the chain of command to someone who can find a gap in the policy or even shift the policy.

You can say to the clerk, "It sounds like it's time for me to speak with the supervisor [or vice-president]."

Along the lines of "be unusual," we notice that the person who has the most behavioral options has an advantage in a negotiation. This reminds me of what author Jeff Salzman said about his mother having an advantage during an argument with his father. They both would slam doors or yell. But when she absolutely needed to win she had one extra "weapon." She could cry. That's it: Jeff's father was defeated.

So to be an Effective Negotiator, do consider doing something unusual.
[By the way, I don't recommend crying during a business situation.]

When you do something unusual, it can be a Pattern Interrupt. For example, some people use the pattern of yelling to gain their way. At times, you can throw off their game by avoiding a response of cowering or yelling back. In this way, the gruff person's pattern has been interrupted. For example, one of my clients, Maxine, responded to an insult by replying: "You know, that tells me something interesting about you." The gruff person replied, "What?" Maxine continued, "You are really concerned about Part 3 of this project. I can respect that. Let's see what we can do to preserve Part 3."

Some of my older relatives like to offer me unsolicited advice. They look at my schedule, offer their advice and conclude: "Tom, you're wrong." And my reply, on occasion, has been, "I'm different."

When I say, "I'm different," I avoid engaging in a head-on conflict. I don't say that the other person is wrong, mean or misguided. I'm doing a Pattern Interrupt.

Point to Remember:

When you do something unusual, you can interrupt the pattern in the other person's behavior. This method can help you take the negotiation into a new direction that can yield your desired result.

Your Action Step:

Preplan how you'll do a Pattern Interrupt if things get intense during a negotiation. What forms of Pattern Interrupt appeal to you?

a) The other person yells, and you reply, "Oh, that tells me something about you." (This phrase is said in a mild tone.)

b) You say, "Oh! I just remembered something. I'll be back in a moment or two."

c) You say, "Really? I haven't thought of it that way. Is there anything else?"

[Here's a vivid example of a Pattern Interrupt. One time I

was in a really tense meeting, and my suit coat sleeve caught on a glass of water. Splash! Water all over the table. That was a real Pattern Interrupt. The other person and I laughed, and the direction of the negotiation changed. The tension was dissipated.]

5) DON'T LET A PERSON'S TITLE STOP YOU FROM ASKING QUESTIONS

Some people feel intimidated in the presence of another person who has a title such as doctor, lawyer, accountant, professor or president. Many people think that these title holders are those entrusted with "sacred knowledge."

The truth is: although these people have some extra learning or expertise, they are still human beings, subject to distraction, memory lapses, biases, prejudices and blind sides.

Do not hesitate to ask for a second (or third) medical opinion if a doctor suggests some radical treatment. Don't let thoughts of "hurting someone's feelings" stop you from getting vital information.

Experts can be wrong. For example, numerous doctors felt that Barry Marshall and Robin Warren were wrong about bacteria causing a certain form of peptic ulcer. The experts did not stop scoffing until Barry Marshall drank H. Pylori bacteria to prove it caused peptic ulcers and got one. He took antibiotics, got better and won (with his colleague Robin Warren) the 2005 Nobel Prize in Physiology or Medicine. It has been reported that this discovery reversed decades of medical doctrine that surmised that ulcers were caused by too much acid, stress, and spicy foods.

My point is: do not let a title or someone's "expert status" prevent you from asking questions. You can say to the expert, "I have a question. I always like learning something."

You may also need to follow your own intuition despite what "experts" say. Walt Disney had to press on through the resistance of his brother and partner Roy O. Disney, the board of directors and Walt's wife, Lillian, who all thought Disneyland would fail. In fact, Walt Disney had to cash in his life insurance to fund the initial development stage of Disneyland. Why? No one had seen a clean theme park before. There had never been such a theme park. Thanks, Walt.

One time I was appalled to hear that a dear friend went to see a doctor about her condition and did not ask the tough questions. It's her body and her health. She told me that she was concerned about "annoying" or "bothering" the doctor. I have worked with students and clients who had similar confusion about the differences between being assertive versus being aggressive. In a negotiation, it is often necessary to be assertive, that is, clearly expressing what you want in a polite but firm manner.

[Here is the polite but firm way to talk with a doctor about your desire for a second opinion: "Thank you for this information. I really appreciate all your efforts. And I'd feel more comfortable with some more information. I'd like a second opinion."]

I once helped a client gain more money for her parents who were being shortchanged by an insurance company representative. I invited her to say, "That is not acceptable. You need to do better than that." She immediately replied, "No, I could not do that." I asked, "Why?" She replied, "Then I would be a b***h." I helped her understand that a polite but firm tone is not aggressive. And the good news is that she did use the assertive phrases ("That is not acceptable. You need to do better than that."), and she gained $300.00 for her parents.

Do not let an expert intimidate you. And do not let your own fear of coming across as "pushy" stop you from getting your fair deal. Ask questions and make assertive statements like: "That's not working for me. How can you keep your good customer happy? [if you're talking to a vendor]"

Point to Remember:
Remember to ask questions of an expert. To ask for something in an assertive way is appropriate.

Your Action Step:
Here are statements and questions you can use:
- I have a question. I always like learning something.
- That's not acceptable. How can you do better than that?
- You'll need to do better than that.
- How does Acme Company keep their customers happy?

6) ADMIT THAT THE OTHER PERSON IS PARTIALLY CORRECT AND THAT YOU MADE AN ERROR

This is one of the most powerful methods I have ever learned. When two people come together, there is a natural tension. Both want to express themselves first. The solution is for you to listen first.

Secondly, people often deeply want "to be right."

So tell the other person in the negotiation, "You're right." And if appropriate, admit a little error on your part. Why? It puts the other person at ease. Often, the person becomes more cooperative and collaborative in negotiating a mutually beneficial resolution.

You could say something like: "You're right. I can be distracted sometimes. I'll try to do better. Let me see if I understood you correctly. You said that the AB-part is the most important. Do I have that about right?"

When you say, "you're right," you take away the negative energy. Many people gear up for a fight or to overwhelm you. Do what Aikido masters do: Avoid resisting and then guide the energy past you. That is, like an Aikido master, you do *not* resist. A form of resistance sounds like: "No, I didn't make a mistake. You have it wrong." Instead, you admit a little error and the other person becomes surprised. Instead of resisting, you are bringing an agreeable tone and energy to the discussion.

Point to Remember:
Remember the other person wants to feel "right." Take this fact and use it to your advantage (when appropriate). You can make a connection by saying, "You're right" and admitting a small error.

Your Action Step:

Quiet down your ego and observe if you've made a small error and say, "You're right about . . ."

7) SAY, "I AGREE," IF APPROPRIATE

Have you noticed a number of people who "always have to be right"? As top entrepreneur Mary Kay Ash said, "Everyone has an invisible sign hanging from their neck saying, 'Make me feel important.' Never forget this message when working with people." When you say, "I agree" to some little point, you release some of the tension in the room. You could say something like: "I agree Part 2 of the project is crucial for the client."

When you say, "I agree," you allow the other person to relax and feel that he or she does not need to push forward an opinion.

So look for something that you do agree about. Most people are poor at acting or pretending, so don't try to pretend you like or agree with something that bothers you. Instead, find something you can sincerely express "I agree" about.

Point to Remember:
People want to be seen as right, so say "I agree," if appropriate.

Your Action Step:
Pay close attention to the person and the whole situation and look for something that you can say "I agree" about.

8) REMEMBER "MORE SWEAT
IN TRAINING, LESS BLOOD IN BATTLE"

Want to get better at negotiating? Rehearse. Practice with small negotiation opportunities. Go to a flea market and practice.

Several years ago, I was giving a speech in New York City. I tend to record my speeches and I needed an audio recorder. So in search of a reasonably priced audio recorder, I walked, with a friend, into a downtown shop (that is, a tourist trap) and a unit was listed as $25.00. I said, "How about $15.00?" to a salesman. He replied with a rude tone and disparaging remarks. I then said, "You might ask your supervisor." More grumpy remarks. So I turned on my heel and guided my friend with me to leave. When we were at the door, the salesman called out, "Wait." And, subsequently, I purchased the audio recorder for $15.00. I thought of this as "good practice."

You need to train yourself to hold your calm in a negotiating situation. Keep looking on each opportunity to negotiate as good practice. As the old phrase goes: "You got to get in the water to swim."

Point to Remember:
Remember, "More sweat in training, less blood in battle."

Your Action Step:
Identify some small situation in which you can practice negotiating—then take action and practice.

9) PEOPLE WHO OBSESS ON THE "EGO-WIN" END UP LOSING

The real prizes in a negotiation are not someone's approval or someone giving up and conceding, "You're right. I was wrong." Those are just trinkets for your ego. People who let their ego get tangled up in a negotiation often lose. What do they lose? Perspective. More importantly, they often lose their opportunity to have their deep goals realized.

Often, one important tactic is to let the other person feel that she has won and done better than you did. Why? You want to keep things feeling comfortable so that you'll be able to have a positive interaction, or negotiation, again in the future.

Small things count. Just as we want the person to feel that she won, we also want the person to feel that we are trustworthy and keep our commitments. For example, several years ago, I loaned a co-worker $20.00. I was amazed when he later forgot the transaction since he was so reliable about business matters. In any case, I wrote the whole thing off because he had taught me some HTML code writing. About twenty years later, I happened to see him in a bookstore in Mountain View, California. And three things jumped into my mind: Good to see you, where did your hair go? and where is my $20.00?

I did not mention the $20.00. I talked about how I visited with him and his wife at the hospital while everyone was worried about his premature baby. He replied, "My son is taller than me now." It was a good interaction.

Actually, he taught me an important lesson: Only loan an amount of money that will not hurt you if it becomes a "gift."

Point to Remember:
Keep your eyes on your deep goals and quiet down your ego.

Your Action Step:
Before the negotiation, write down your real goals. At various points during the negotiation, review your list to keep yourself on track.

10) BE POLITE, BUT FIRM

If you lose your cool, it is easy for the other person to write you off as unreasonable or plain crazy.

Stay polite, but firm. In a pleasant tone, you can say:
- Well, it looks like it's time for me to talk with a supervisor.
- Are you telling me, I can't talk with a supervisor?
- So how does [Company Name] keep good customers happy?

Even when you're polite, you'll likely run into situations when it's better to end a phone interaction. Why? Because you may do better by calling later and talking with a different representative on the phone. I have also twice found it necessary to call at a different time to talk with a different supervisor. Again, you can say politely, "Oh, something has come up here. I'll need to go. Have a good day. Goodbye." Then wait a number of hours and call back in hopes of connecting with a different representative.

Point to Remember:
Be polite, but firm.

Your Action Step:
Preplan your interaction. Write down your own script. Choose sentences that are polite, but firm. Be sure also to rehearse saying the words out loud.

CONCLUSION TO BOOK III:
10 GENERAL PRINCIPLES OF EFFECTIVE NEGOTIATING

We have covered a number of principles and specific actions. Remember: merely reading these details is a modest value compared to the huge value you get from rehearsing. By rehearsing, you make the methods part of you. Negotiation happens in real time. You need lots of options so you can adapt well.

In *BOOK IV: Use Strategies to Make Yourself Stronger (The Strong Can Negotiate Effectively)*, we will discuss eleven topics and some surprising applications for your next negotiation.

Let's move forward . . .

BOOK IV: USE 12 STRATEGIES TO MAKE YOURSELF STRONGER (THE STRONG CAN NEGOTIATE EFFECTIVELY)

Negotiation is a mix of principles, strategies and rehearsal. I first explored the following topics on my blog at www.BeHeardandBeTrusted.com.

The Topics:
1) Is it Fear or Your Heart-Focus? Get Yourself Moving Forward!
2) Unleash Your Full Strength and Succeed!
3) Create Wow! in Your Life
4) Imagine Expressing Your Voice, Your Heart—and Being Heard!
5) What Does It Really Take to Improve Your Life?
6) When Is It Your time?
7) How to Unleash Your Greatness
8) How You Can Stand Out, Express Your Personal Brand and Welcome Success

9) Tired of Feeling Stuck? How to Release Yourself to a Better Life

10) Need Some Relief? Bring Humor and Laughter into Your Life

11) Feel You Have No Time? Here's What You Can Do

12) How You Can Radiate Charisma with Your Next Speech

1) IS IT FEAR OR YOUR HEART-FOCUS? GET YOURSELF MOVING FORWARD

"Why can't I get myself to do the tough work?" Tabitha asked her sister Libby. "Am I afraid? Is fear stopping me?" Good questions. How about you? Are you feeling stuck? Have you looked around and asked, "Why haven't I done better by now?"

Now, we'll take a great step forward by excavating what may be really going on for you so that you take a leap forward for success. Toward that end, we'll use the L.O.O.K. process:

L – Listen
O – Open
O – Overlook
K – Kindle

1. Listen
The first step is starting with questions, including:
- Is there something that I'm afraid of that is holding me back?

A truly strong person can pause for a moment and see if

he or she is vulnerable and has allowed some form of fear to stop real progress and personal growth.

Here's another important question:

Could it be that it's not fear that's holding you back? It may be that your heart is not in what you're doing.

So it will take courage for you to answer the following questions for yourself. And the payoff is that you will have a springboard to a new level of success and fulfillment:

- Why are you doing this action?
- If you're not doing what you "should do," what's holding you back?
- What would you rather be doing?
- Would you do this for free—that is, if you weren't getting paid?
- If you didn't have to earn a living, would you be doing this?
- Where is the joy in just doing this? (separate this from a monetary benefit.)
- What do you want to feel while doing this?
- What do you expect you'll feel once you accomplish this?

My clients find it helpful to write their answers in a personal journal. As you write, you "open the space" so you can listen to your heart. The process helps you slow down and hear yourself. (You could also talk this over with a trusted friend. Some of my clients record their comments to listen to later.)

Why is this important?

When your heart is engaged, you have access to a lot of energy; you jump over the hurdles and press through the barriers.

2. Open

If you're going to make real progress, you'll need to be open in your approach to examining your assumptions and perceptions about what seems to be going on in your life now.

The phrases "I'm not afraid" and "Been there. It didn't work" can hold you back.

They can keep you stuck. Why? They are like blinders on a horse; they prevent you from seeing other possibilities on the periphery. Have you noticed that some people just keep getting what they expect to get? Here's one reason that this occurs. If they don't expect to get more, they are unlikely to develop new steps and devote better efforts to getting good results.

But this is not for you. You'll need to be open to doing something differently so you can gain a new perspective. Perhaps talking with a coach or counselor will help you uncover subconscious conditioning that hinders you.

3. Overlook

When we're talking about "overlook" we mean to "look over" or "look beyond" your current beliefs and assumptions.

We also need to overlook the past—that is, look beyond your past experience. Some people say, "I know this because I already did that in the past." These individuals seem to "need to be right" so much that they're willing to talk themselves out of a bright new future.

To look beyond the past, we need you to engage with the present moment.

Ask questions like:

- What's going on now—in this present moment?
- What am I feeling?
- Does something feel off?
- Does something seem like the tip of an iceberg?
- What do I feel good about in my present life?

4. Kindle

Kindle, that is, nurture the flame of your energy and intuition.

I'm talking about "kindling your heart-focus."

At various times, I have heard college students' concern about whether to pursue additional education or certain job paths.

Here are some principles that can be used to take yourself to a new level of success and fulfillment:

- *Focus on doing something that really engages your heart.* Why? Because if you love it, you'll put more time and effort into it—so you become one of the best at that form of work. (For example, I write every day. I simply like to write. Sure, when writing a book or screenplay, I must do a number of revisions and, at times, that's drudgery. But I often have a good time while writing.)

- *Whatever you do for earning a living, be sure to have some project that you control.* Why? In particular, if you're an artist who works for clients, you may find yourself burning out. What's the reason? The client (or boss) has all the power and you may find that the leader makes the wrong decisions and takes the project away before you can bring it to a level of excellence that you would feel great about. Instead, at home, devote some time to your own project. You'll control when it is done. You set your own criteria of what makes the work rise to the level of excellence.

- *"Book yourself into your own studio."* I know a number of people who purchased a lot of music equipment (synthesizers, mixing board, software, etc.). They decided that they must form a recording studio to make some money with the equipment. Over the years, I have asked, "Do you book yourself each week into your own studio?" And they reply, "No. I'm too busy recording other people's stuff." That's tragic! Be sure to make time for your own artwork. You'll experience more happy moments.

So let's take a moment and realize that your hesitation (or even procrastination) may be from fear—or perhaps, from your heart not being in the work itself.

Use this section's questions as a springboard for self-knowledge. Get access to your intuition. Discover your wellspring of energy.

Some Thoughts about Fear, Heart-Focus and Negotiation

To negotiate at your best, you need to be fully engaged with your heartfelt goals. Why are you really negotiating? What do you desire to feel upon gaining what you want?

We do things for many reasons. I just heard of the niece of a friend who was applying for medical school just because she was a whiz at biology research. Whoa! Perhaps, she'd rather be a researcher/professor than a doctor. So write down your goals for the negotiation and then take time to get a heart-focus about them. Your list could look something like my client Joey's list:

- I want to get a good price for my used car.
- Why?
- I need the money.
- Why?
- I have to eat.
- Any other reason?
- I want to take my girlfriend to dinner and a movie.
- Why?
- I want us to have some good times. We have been irritable with each other recently.
- Anything else?
- I want to show her that I'm good with money.
- Why?
- I don't want to lose her.
- Anything else?
- I don't want to feel lonely ever again.

It takes some effort to get to our heart-focus.

Now that Joey knows that getting a good price for his used car is related to how he feels about his relationship with his girlfriend, he can take that energy and apply it to studying the material in this book and rehearsing before the negotiation.

2) UNLEASH YOUR FULL STRENGTH AND SUCCEED!

"Tell the truth. Have you put your full strength into this? Or have you been half-hearted about it?" Janet asked her sister Sarah. Just imagine if you could get access to your full strength. What could you get done? How would success rush in for you? To help you get access to your full strength, we'll use the F.U.L.L. process:

F – Focus
U – Unleash
L – Look
L – Lock in

1. Focus

How are many people stuck? They've allowed their energy to be dissipated. It takes focusing your attention to make a leap forward. I know someone who has talked about writing a book for 11 years . . . but somehow organizing the house keeps coming up as more important. To motivate me to write a screenplay or a book, I keep a log next to my computer monitor of how many words I write each day. Bestselling author John Grisham says, "You're not serious unless you write 1,000 words a day." I'll add that even with 100 words a day, you'll still make progress. In order to focus on your dreams, you must keep them right in front of your eyes. How? Write down your goal and review it often. Take a step forward each day.

2. Unleash

Unleash your energy. This sounds like a good idea. The question is: how do you release the energy that is hidden inside you?

I'll illustrate this with a personal example. It took steady effort during nearly two years to complete my new book *Full Strength Marketing* (co-authored with Linda L. Chappo). Now that the book is on Amazon.com and is selling, I'm enjoying a dream come true. How did I keep up my energy level? I started with a vision. And that's the way to release the energy that is hidden inside you.

I imagined that the book would help a single mother who either has a business or is considering starting a business. That's what gets hope and excitement going for me. To unleash my energy, my question (for myself) is "Who am I going to help? And how am I going to help that person?"

Another way to unleash energy is to answer this question: "Where is the joy?" A number of my graduate students take a journey to find out what truly brings them joy. A student starts with aspirations to be an animator but discovers that she has more skill and enjoyment in modeling the character. (Modeling is the process of constructing a character's appearance by using advanced software.) Or the other way around. The point is that you need to enjoy doing the work, not just having completed the work. When you enjoy the work, you naturally devote more time and effort to improving your skills. And you do better work. So success arrives naturally.

3. Look

Look for how other people have made successful efforts in your industry or art form. I remember when my father was trying to learn how to ride a unicycle. I suggested that he get a coach. When I decide to learn something, I often hire an expert to teach exactly what I need to know. The crucial question is: "What is the most important thing I need to know about this topic?"

But my father never hired a coach, and he never learned to ride that unicycle.

My father's stubbornness about not seeking guidance from a coach stands out for me as a big warning. No coach equals no big progress . . . and one eventually gives up.

But this is not for you. Identify what you need to learn and find the most efficient way to learn it.

Efficiency is important. My sweetheart endures her dyslexia. Her solution is to listen to audio books. Here's another example: one of my top team members is a slow reader. We're both clear that he simply does not like to read. So I make sure that he can attend a staged reading of a screenplay. That's when he really learns what he needs to know about the script.

4. Lock in

To be strong and get things done, you need to lock some things in place. In leading my team and also teaching seven graduate-level/college classes, I'm busy. And I find it necessary to "lock in" disciplined efforts. For example, I use "15 Days, 15 Minutes." That means that each day, I write for 15 minutes no matter what. Often I'll write upon first awakening in the morning. You can apply this to physical fitness or painting or whatever you wish to pursue.

Another part of "lock in" is in setting schedules. One author noted that true entrepreneurs set "get this done" goals as opposed to vague thoughts like "I'll work on the book today, and see how far I get." A "get this done" goal can be: "I'll write a two-page workshop proposal and send it to that organization today." A goal like this helps in two ways: a) one avoids the temptation to work on the proposal for weeks and b) no one wants to read more than two pages, anyway.

So "lock in" is not only about what you are going to do, it's also about what you choose not to do.

Sometimes, it seems that popular culture is encouraging people to be "dabblers." Even formal education has us dabble in math, science, and language. I feel fortunate that during my grammar school years, I was allowed to excel through a program and learn to read many levels above my grade level. You see, I was not dabbling in reading. I become quite proficient at it and currently read up to 85 books in one year.

So I encourage you to focus your energy and avoid merely "dabbling." Be sure to unleash your full strength to develop the success you desire.

Some Thoughts about Your Full Strength and Negotiation:

You can't put in half-hearted efforts if you want to succeed in the negotiation. When your heart is fully engaged, you will put in the time and effort to be fully prepared. An important part of preparation is to develop an "If – then" List of Actions. Here's an example: "If the other person won't commit to delivery in five days, then I will request a discount of 25%." Another way to prepare is write down a list of *10 Tough Questions*. I often call these questions the ones "you don't want to answer." Come up with two answers per tough question. That's right. You'll have 20 answers (this will form your second list entitled *20 Answers*). And you'll usually be a lot better prepared than most people.

3) CREATE WOW! IN YOUR LIFE

Have you ever felt choked by duties and routines? Have you started some things that have descended into boredom? Here we'll talk about bringing up your energy level and helping you reconnect with the dreams residing in your heart. We need to create W.O.W. in our lives.

W – wake up
O – open
W – wish

1. Wake up

When we allow ourselves to overwork and become exhausted, we become zombies propped up by coffee and sugar. One time I was exhausted and I talked with an elderly relative. A bit of compassion and wisdom would have been refreshing. Instead, he brusquely said, "You do your duty."

When you really aim to wake up about the reality of your life, you're likely to find that "conventional wisdom" is inadequate. When my relative said, "You do your duty," I surprised myself when I replied: "I do my duty and it's not making me happy." Clearly, doing my duty was not enough.

That was a true Wake up! moment for me.

Now, I invite you to wake up and see if you dropped any dreams along the way. Recently, on my blog BeHeardandBeTrusted.com, I featured a poster to my upcoming feature film series entitled *TimePulse*. I wrote my first draft of *TimePulse* when I was 14 years old. I have been working on it steadily. . . and I invite you to find something that keeps you smiling and full of energy.

In talking about smiling, I'm also referring to happiness. A number of researchers and authors note that making happiness as one's primary goal can cause trouble. Why? Because happiness is truly a by-product of living a life of personal growth and making a contribution to making life better for other people.

Along the line of making life better for others, I recall an old phrase: "Happiness is something to do, someone to love and something to hope for." Well, something to do and someone to love involves a lot of "maintenance" efforts. You know, washing dishes, cleaning clothes, and cleaning the cat box. When I was stuck in the pattern of "do my duty/not making me happy," I didn't have something to look forward to every day.

You don't need something big to happen. It can be small things. For example, I'm writing this book and listening to music. I'm happy.

So what do you have to look forward to today? Will you take a couple of moments to enjoy some tea while gazing out a window? Will you enjoy the brief walk from your office to public transportation? Pay attention: life is in the "small" moments.

By the way, having something to look forward to creates good energy in you and those around you. I know a couple of people who do not have things to look forward to. These people are like sinkholes of energy. For example, negative people's complaining can take our mood down. I limit my exposure to them.

Be an energy creator. Give yourself something to look forward to—and people will look forward to being in your presence.

I want to share with you the power of "Wow!" When I first saw the poster *TimePulse* as rendered by a team member, I immediately wrote 7,639 words for one of the screenplays. I was that excited. What fills you with energy and excitement?

2. Open

You can't get anything new in your life if you won't open the door. You also need to open up space in your life. If your life is already packed, you need to toss a couple of things aside to make space for something new. As I mentioned, I use a process I call "15-15"—that is, 15 Days, 15 Minutes. I place these fifteen minutes early in my day so that I am certain to do something important and that generates life-energy.

3. Wish

Some of us are nearly choked by our goals. How? We're living in a future of "It'll be better when I get this done," or "When I don't have to endure that anymore. . ."

But some magic has been lost. When I said "nearly choked," I'm referring to feeling trapped in a life of drudgery and routine and feeling like we can't breathe. What happened to our fondest wishes?

Kids do something quite well: they wish for what they want. Unfortunately, I know a number of adults who have simply given up on wishing for anything. Along those lines, I remember this quote:

If you have built castles in the air, your work need not be lost; that is where they should be. Now put the foundations under them. - Henry David Thoreau

Thirty-four years ago, I began with a wish: a wish to tell a story that I now call *TimePulse*. Since I wrote the first draft at 14, I have directed films, had a feature film go to the Cannes Film market, written 19 books now on Amazon.com (one book went to #1 on Amazon.com in Hot New Releases in Business Life), and have given speeches at Stanford University and cities across the United States. I've taught thousands of graduate students/college students.

But I never let go of my *TimePulse* wish.

And I have been building the foundations: I'm a much better writer and storyteller 34 years later.

Now, I invite you to dust off your wishes. When you want Wow! in your life, remember:

W – wake up
O – open
W – wish

To have Wow! in your life, you need to open up time and space in your life for new experiences. For example, in my research for my book *Darkest Secrets of Persuasion and Seduction Masters* (the first book in this series), I uncovered that romantic couples bring romance to their relationship by, wait for it, sharing new experiences. You need to make your wishes and hopes (for new experiences like vacations, etc.) known to yourself and your partner.

I have a friend who has his life revolve around comfort. And that's what he gets.
He doesn't understand that taking appropriate risks opens the door to joy and fulfillment.
But this is not for you.
Live a little.
No!—better than that: Live a lot!
And allow yourself to realize that this is an "And" life.

You can do your duty, AND you can make space for activities that bring a smile to your face each day.

Some Thoughts about Create Wow! and Negotiation

If you have Wow! in your life, you have the energy to stand up for yourself. You've got something worth fighting for!

The people who find life boring or a tremendous burden

have a big disadvantage when negotiating. Energized people have more resources. They can be more creative in the moment. Bored or burdened people may also become physically ill. A number of researchers discuss psychoneuroimmunology and notice how the mind, body and spirit truly are connected. When you want to be good at negotiation, you also want to be healthy in mind, body and spirit. You'll be strong on multiple levels. And that's what being effective at negotiation calls for.

4) IMAGINE EXPRESSING YOUR VOICE, YOUR HEART—AND BEING HEARD!

Ever have a BIG problem and wish you had someone to call? Roger Ebert, the film critic, can no longer talk, but he can express his voice. How? He writes his blog, articles, and books. Where do you express your voice? My interviews with successful people have shown that they succeed in a great part because they express their voice in some way. Toward that end, we'll use the C.A.N. process:

C – Close the gap
A – Arrange listening first
N – Notice

1. Close the gap

When we talk with someone, there is a gap, a sense of separation. We try to bridge that gap with words—but they're only symbols. Sometimes, the words (as symbols) mean something different (to the listener) than what we intend. It helps when both people ask gentle questions to be sure that the meaning becomes clear and that the message we sent was accurately received. In this way we build that real bridge from one person to another. The bridge is made of the perception that we are heard and valued because of our essence as a person.

For example, on weekends, I often call some friends who live great distances from me. I call just to "catch up" and ask, "How are things going for you?" By reaching out, asking a question and listening, I begin to close the gap. The tone of my voice and my persistent efforts to hear my friend out all contribute to my closing the gap.

2. Arrange listening first

Do you want someone to truly listen to you? Here's the method. Listen first. When two people meet, they're both wanting to be the first to express their ideas, feelings, insights, complaints, and perhaps, hopes. When you want someone to truly listen to you, listen to the other person first. Then the energy of "I've got to say what's on my mind!" will dissipate. After being heard first, many people (during a networking event) will feel an urge to be reciprocal and will likely (eventually) say, "So what do you do?" or "How are you doing?"

I teach my graduate students the primary three words of networking: "Help them first."

Some people think, "How can I help someone who is so much further ahead in this industry than I am?" The answer is: "Listen to the person." That is both a kindness and a service. Few people get to be an instructor or mentor. People often feel terrific when they're teaching or explaining something. Give the person the chance to express herself. She'll feel better, and you may learn something and gain a friend.

3. Notice

In order to express your voice, your truth, you need to notice what's inside you. How are you feeling? Pause. Check in with yourself. At this moment, I'm feeling great. I'm writing. I'm expressing my voice. Have you expressed your voice today? This week? If not, you have homework. Pull out a personal journal or day planner to schedule some actions.

With your day planner open, consider some ways to express your voice:
1) You call friends to "catch up."
2) You listen and ask questions to learn more.
3) You give a little spontaneous gift to a loved one.
4) You do some form of art (crafts, a song, a poem, cooking, writing in your journal, something else).
5) You express compassion in some way.

In recent years, I learned something important about compassion. We want it directed toward us. We want someone to express compassion toward us for the hardship that we endure. And compassion calls for two things: courage and energy. Why? Because to express compassion, we need to take on a bit of someone's pain (even for just a couple of moments).

Many times in my life, I have had people merely deny my pain because they couldn't (or wouldn't) take on a bit of it. When a family member or a close friend "leaves us hanging," that hurts. On the other hand, when you listen to someone and are really present, then you're expressing a form of compassion.

So now, I'm asking you to notice two things: where you need compassion and where someone near you needs compassion.

When I saw Roger Ebert's "talk" [he had people reading his words] at a TED conference [http://mashable.com/2011/03/05/roger-ebert-ted-talk/], I noticed that he frequently expressed his voice—that is, his closeness with his wife—by reaching for her hand. You can express your voice with other than words. It can be simple: reaching for a loved one's hand or hugging or a smile.

So be sure you express your "voice" (your truth, your heart). This world needs to hear you.

Some Thoughts on Being Heard and Listening—and Negotiation

Many people approach negotiation, like other things in their life, with impatience. That can get them in big trouble. It's better to be strong and patient and hear out the other side first. When two people get together there is often tension in that both people want to express their opinions and feelings first. Fine. Let the other person go first.

Do you want to be a good negotiator? Practice becoming a good listener. First you need to get **3 Listening Blockers** out of your way. The blockers include (as I mentioned earlier in this book):

1) Judging
We judge things all of the time. "Yes, she's right." "No, he's wrong." The solution is to put our judgment on hold in

our mind, and ask a gentle follow-up question.

2) Defending

People say, "No! I don't always forget to take out the garbage. I took it out last Tuesday!" It takes practice to ask, "Is there anything else?" Instead of cutting off the other person, it helps to ask a couple of questions to help the person complete expressing their feelings.

3) Me, too—One Up

Sometimes, we might say something like, "Yes. I can understand. I have three children [when the person was complaining about their one child]." At first glance, it seems like we're sympathizing or even empathizing with the person's situation. But when we "one up," we're turning the spotlight (of the conversation) back upon ourselves. The person is now metaphorically in the dark, and he or she does not like that! When you catch yourself doing "me, too—one up", pause and ask a gentle question. Turn that conversation spotlight back upon the other person.

When you make a connection with the other person, you are likely to complete a negotiation in which you meet your primary goals.

5) WHAT DOES IT REALLY TAKE TO IMPROVE YOUR LIFE?

"When is my life going to get better?!" Carolyn lamented to her friend Trina. So what does it take to truly improve your life? Sitting with the uncomfortable. What? To sit with the uncomfortable means to pause long enough to observe the reality of your situation and then form a plan and take action to create better in your life.

To change, you need energy. When you stop to really feel the discomfort, you're building up an "energy potential." People tend to only change when they're in enough pain that makes changing less painful than sitting in a stuck place.

You and I know that people don't change until they're really ready. And not one moment earlier. To prepare you for positive change, explore the following W.I.N. process.

W – Wonder
I – Intensify
N – Nurture

1. Wonder
It begins with "What can be better than this?" If you don't hold even the slightest hope for something better in life, you won't put any attention or effort toward improvements in your life. I have a friend who is brilliant writer. But she just does not make sure to sit in the seat and write! I've heard her habitual excuses. She doesn't think she can make money at writing. How about making a life while writing? Some poets make no money at writing, but they have a smile on their face every day. Isn't that worth something? I always remember that author Joseph Campbell said, "I don't believe people are looking for the meaning of life as much as they are looking for the experience of being alive."

Do you want to feel alive? It will first require a thought filled with wonder and hope. And, yes, it will then take action—to step forth out of your comfort zone.

2. Intensify

You need to make a space—a hole in your busyness to feel your feelings. And you'll need to feel the discomfort so that you'll be sufficiently motivated to take action. In my book, *Nothing Can Stop You This Year!* (free chapter on Amazon.com at http://bit.ly/8zQywm), I begin by sharing the time I saw a man die before my eyes. He was years younger than me and he was a motorcyclist struck by a jeep. He died, and my mind was filled with the phrase: "I want to live!" And I took action and ended a seven-year relationship, moved, and dove deeply into my lifework.

From my above example, we notice that life sometimes intensifies our experience. We start to feel emotions that we haven't felt before. We start thinking about primal details like life, death, the meaning of one's life, and love. We even consider, "Have I missed the important parts of life?"

Similarly, I was confronted with some tough realizations when I faced surgery. The hospital's form stated that something could go wrong . . . sign here. So I put my affairs in order. I updated my Last Will and Testament and wrote my directive of care if something went wrong in the operating room. I chose to use this situation as an opportunity (yes, opportunity) to face my mortality. By the way, I made a decision that in the days just before the operation, I didn't want to rush around getting more done. [This was the opposite of author Isaac Asimov's comment: "If my doctor told me I had only six months to live, I wouldn't brood. I'd type a little faster."] What I wanted was calm and peace. I brought myself to a place of acceptance. I contacted people important to me and expressed my love and appreciation.

My point is that you can use a crisis or something painful when you choose to sit with the discomfort and find out what is on the opposite side of the door. You can intensify your experience of life. You intensify your awareness of the truth of your life. Some of that truth is that something is uncomfortable. You can only heal and improve what you're aware of.

3. Nurture

Enlightenment. Is it possible? From listening to my clients' experiences, I can say a resounding, "Yes!" And there is an important detail. You must put effort into holding onto what you learn. Writing in a journal can help. Talking about what you learned can help, too. In my book *10 Seconds to Wealth: Master the Moment by Using Your Divine Gifts*, I write about your *Divine Aha!*—that's the experience in life when you say, "Aha! Now I understand." You need to actually nurture yourself, your feelings, and your retention of what you learn. Why? Because daily life is so distracting!

Each day, I seem to mention to a friend or family member something like: "Aren't those trees pretty? I like walking in this park. Walking on the frozen tundra in Antarctica would sure be different."

My point is that the art of life is much about the art of appreciating your gifts in the here and now.

Yes!—you can improve your life. Remember, it often calls for sitting with the uncomfortable and building up energy to take appropriate action . . . and, then you take that appropriate action.

Then, you'll have that breathtaking experience of "Wow! I feel really alive."

Some Thoughts on "What does it really take to improve your life?"—and Negotiation

Earlier, I mentioned a powerful question: "What can be better than this?" All improvement begins with a certain level of dissatisfaction. For example, I have a friend whose aim in life has been. . . wait for it . . . comfort. So he doesn't stretch himself. He works at a job that has nothing to do with his college degree. No fully committed romantic relationship for him. Why? Because a fully committed relationship demands much from each partner. To gain fulfillment, you need to devote focused effort and you need to endure uncertainty and some pain. Anyone who has had a long-term relationship is acquainted with some uncertainty and some pain. But it's worth it! Why? Because you feel really alive! The lows are tough to endure, but the highs are joyous.

The same thing goes for negotiation. You need commitment to preparation and rehearsal. You need to practice holding your calm and resolve during any negotiation. I invite you to connect with what will enliven you and make your heart sing. From this wellspring, you'll have the energy to negotiate well.

6) WHEN IS IT *YOUR* TIME?

Have you ever said, "I don't have time to take a break"? If you don't have time to take a brief break, you likely feel overcommitted to other people's requirements for your time.

I have a question for you: When is it your time? You might reply: "To do what?" To enjoy life, to shine, to leap forward, to succeed, to relax, and to feel inner peace. To open the door for you to feel true fulfillment, let's explore the T.I.M.E. process:

T – Tap in
I – Intuit
M – Measure
E – Enjoy

1. Tap in

Imagine that life is a crystal clear waterfall of refreshing water. And you feel parched. All you need to do is "tap in" and have your fill of the water. But why don't we do it? Why do we hesitate to do anything? Fear.

A number of successful people I've talked with told me about a time when they felt fear but moved forward on their goals anyway. They pressed through the fear.

You have a choice in each moment. You could allow fear to sound like "Stop!" On the other hand, you could choose to interpret fear as a signal or reminder. Fear can be a reminder that sounds like: "Okay. This is important to you. Stay aware. Get coaching. Make this work. It's worth it."

You have a hidden natural brilliance. How will you know what it is unless you stretch and try something new? And often, as a companion, fear shows up. Okay.

Everything that means so much to me has required that I

take an appropriate risk.

Ask yourself: What appropriate risk stands before me now?

What hidden elements of my natural brilliance might arise if I step out of my comfort zone?

Tap into your true self—the source of your natural brilliance.

2. Intuit

Let's not deceive ourselves. You know what you need, but you may have shut down emotionally.

Let me demonstrate this:

- Jeannie knows (in her heart) that she wants to be a writer; but fear of ridicule has her make excuses (like "I don't have the time.")
- Sam knows (in his heart) that he wants to be an actor; but fear of failure has him avoiding auditions.

How do you deal with fear? First, admit it exists, and then get help and get coaching. For example, I have two editors for every book I write.

When you feel some form of fear, pause. Make sure you make space to listen to your intuition.

Intuition says: "Expand. Try an experiment."

Fear says: "Contract. Hide."

When is it your time?

Now is your time! Listen to your intuition and take that empowering action.

3. Measure

How do you know you made any progress toward your goals today? You measure it. You keep score. How?

Here are examples:
- Many authors do five things a day to promote their book.
- Many authors use the word-count option in their word processing program to keep track of their progress and keep up their own morale.
- A number of people I know count how many sit-ups, pushups, etc. they do each day.

Okay, I admit. Sometimes, I do my daily push-ups, sit-ups and more, only because I will be glad to record my healthy actions in my *Daily Journal of Victories and Blessings*. Yes, it's another victory over inertia.

This is your time. Take steps toward fulfilling your goals each day. Log them. Reward yourself. In the final analysis, you must be your own best coach (whether you have a coach or not).

4. Enjoy

I know some people who do not think that enjoyment is a valuable part of living. Well, that's sad for them. They are truly missing out. They probably don't realize that a person who enjoys life is fun to be around. This is an important distinction. If you are uncomfortable with yourself, you can put people on edge. That can disrupt your getting good results in a negotiation.

The truth is: people who are comfortable with themselves are easy to be around.

A charismatic person often makes the listener feel like she's the most important person in the building. I know some people who metaphorically "wear a martyr's badge" — that means, they act as if they are special for sacrificing for everyone else. The person wearing the "martyr's badge" often tends to be irritable and to lash out at others. But this is not for you.

Be sure to do something each day that brings a smile and laughter to your life. Think of it as a sacred duty — no, better than that: it's a sacred opportunity. How? If you're good to yourself, it's more likely that you'll have the energy to be good to others.

Remember the answer to *when is it your time?*

Now is your time. This is the only time you have. Do something today that is in the direction of your highest good. And you'll discover that in expressing your hidden natural brilliance, you're giving exactly what this world needs.

Some Thoughts about "When is it *Your* Time?" — and Negotiation

To negotiate well, you must be strong. And you need to have some feelings of happiness and fulfillment. That's related to what I mean about "your time." As I wrote above, be sure to do something each day that brings a smile and laughter to your life. In this way, you create positive energy. You'll need that energy to retain your composure when things get difficult in a negotiation. In addition, someone who smiles and laughs each day just moves with a comfortable energy. Charismatic people exude such a comfortable energy and put everyone at ease around them. In a negotiation, the charismatic person who sets the other at ease tends to get what he or she really wants.

7) HOW TO UNLEASH YOUR GREATNESS

Do you have greatness hidden in you?

First, let me illustrate this. "The great inventions of humankind," I said to my graduate students, "The wheel, the light bulb and Puffs—you get somewhere, you can see where you're going, and you go in comfort." My graduate students chuckled about the Puffs (tissues) comment.

Now, I shared the above comment because it's amusing and memorable. In addition, I'm making a point: greatness does not need to be only the big world-changing material. I'm wearing headphones now so I can type and not disturb sleeping family members. So at this moment, I feel that the makers of headphones are "great."

About greatness: there's something that only you can bring to this world. What is it? Toward discovering your answer, let's use the Y.E.S. process:

Y – Yearn
E – Express
S – Story-tell

1. Yearn

What do you truly want? You can use your true desires as a source for your greatness.

Many people I have met are paralyzed by fear in some form. I have a brilliant friend who lives in a backwater town and does not move to where the high-end jobs are. His house is paid for and it would be disruptive to move. Still, he keeps on complaining.

I have another friend who is a terrific writer, but she does not schedule daily time to write. She also does not hire an editor to help her raise her writing to the level at which it would be publishable (through self-publishing or through a conventional publisher).

To overcome fear, you need to really yearn. You must want it so much that you are moved to transcend fear. I know many talented people. Only a small number of these individuals want something with intensity enough to do all the work and withstand all the necessary pain to get what they want to blossom in the world.

I remember Stephen King's comment: "Talent is cheaper than table salt. What separates the talented individual from the successful one is a lot of hard work." I'll add that, in writing, success requires good editing and lots of revisions.

Now, it's your turn. Do you know exactly what you want? Ask yourself.

Here's my personal response to the question of what do you want?:

"I want to help people to experience enthusiasm, love and wisdom to fulfill big dreams."

Here are some specifics of what outcomes I want:
- Readers all over the world enhance their success and fulfillment through my 18 books on Amazon.com
- Children smile and enjoy laughter through my *Crystal Pegasus* book and subsequent animated feature film (and toys and later TV series).
- Science fiction fans feel energized and inspired while reading my book *TimePulse*. Later, they will enjoy the subsequent graphic novels and trilogy of feature films of my *TimePulse* science fiction franchise.

Why do I work so much? Because it feels exciting and fulfilling to make a positive contribution to the lives of people worldwide.

So now it's your turn. Take one minute and write down your answer to the question: "What do you want?" Remember to connect with your feelings as you write down the specifics related to your desires.

2. Express
The path to expressing your greatness begins with writing down three forms of effective goals. Why? Because you need to connect with your feelings related to the reasons for your goals.

Golden "Pull" Goals
These are your "moving toward" goals. Perhaps you want to fund college for your daughter. Maybe you want to have a lovely house or take joyful vacations around the world. Or

maybe you truly want to make a contribution to other people. In essence, these goals pull you forward. They are attractive and warm.

Dark Boot Goals

I use the phrase Dark Boot Goals because they involve pain. The metaphor is having a boot hit your rear end and propel you forward. In talking with certain clients, I notice that some are consumed with these Dark Boot Goals. Basically, they are trying to "keep their head above water." These goals are known as "moving away from" goals. That is, you're trying to move away from something that can cause you pain. A prime example would be doing your tax paperwork to avoid tax penalties.

The truth is that many of us (when we absolutely must do something) are motivated by pain. Specifically, the avoidance of pain. For example, some people only do housework to avoid the pain of feeling embarrassed when friends visit and see a messy house.

Many years ago, I preferred to talk only of positive goals. But then I learned that many effective people use the energy of pain to get themselves moving into action. For example, a number of successful people I have interviewed talk about how they use deadlines and the desire to avoid disappointing people as effective motivators. I say: Use what works.

Green Tranquility Goals

These are daily "being" goals, that is, the plan is to live many moments each day as a happy, productive individual. Such "goals" (or daily activities) can include enjoying laughter, getting outside near trees, exercising and enjoying quiet time.

I know some people who are caught up in Golden Pull Goals and Dark Boot Goals and they are not enjoying their lives. This is *not* for you. Instead, add Green Tranquility Goals. I refer to "Green" because it's about growing and blossoming. Imagine if you wanted plants to grow in your garden but you denied them daily sun and water. Be sure to provide enjoyable moments to yourself each day. It doesn't take a lot of time. Fifteen or twenty minutes on a daily basis will brighten your life.

3. Story-tell

We need to be careful about the stories we tell ourselves. Do we frame something as a failure or as a stepping stone? A lashing or a learning experience?

How you tell stories to yourself is crucial. If you tell vivid negative stories, it's like you've removed a plug in the sink. Your positive energy metaphorically goes down the drain.

Instead, you need to enhance your personal energy. If you don't radiate positive energy, people will not be attracted to team up with you.

On the other hand, if you keep up your own energy, you have the ability to pull people in. Then the next step is to tell an effective story to the person you're talking with.

What makes a good story? It includes these elements: problem, tension, suspense, solution and triumphant ending. Here is the important element of the triumphant ending: Find a way to make it include a positive benefit for the person you're talking with.

Being a good storyteller can help you pull together a team or sell your product/service.

The end of your story works well when the listener can imagine how he or she will enjoy a triumphant resolution to a situation.

This last skill is about opening the door to your hidden greatness. How? To stretch and express our full potential we need the cooperation of other people. Even loners who like to work alone often need to ace a job interview to get hired and get the office that they want to hide in.

Anyone who wants more success and fulfillment will do better by applying the Y.E.S. process:

Y – Yearn
E – Express
S – Story-tell

Make this day the first step in your grand and delightful new chapter of life.

Some Thoughts on Unleashing Your Greatness—and Negotiation

As I mentioned, you need to know what you want. Before you engage in a negotiation, be sure to write down your goals. Then, go deeper. Identify all three types of goals: Golden "Pull" Goals, Dark Boot Goals and Green Tranquility Goals. Then, throughout the negotiation review your written goals. During a negotiation new information arises and on occasion, painful things arise, too. Be careful not to fall into the trap novice negotiators trip into: letting feelings and one's ego take over.

Return to your heart-focus by reviewing all three levels of goals. Then you'll be connected with your true and positive inner power.

8) HOW YOU CAN STAND OUT, EXPRESS YOUR PERSONAL BRAND AND WELCOME SUCCESS

"To stand out, find out what you stand for," I said to my graduate students, many of them nervous about getting a job in a tough economy. To gain a job or to gain business, you need to stand out. What's the process? Develop your personal brand, especially to make big success happen for you in this year.

For years, I have guided audiences and clients in developing a personal brand. In fact, the San Francisco Examiner reported me as "The Personal Branding Instructor."

Your personal brand is your answer to: "What are you best known for?"

Your personal brand also basically answers these questions that a potential employer (or customer) has:
- Who are you?
- How can you help me?
- Why can I trust you?

Your personal brand is your promise of excellent performance.

Your personal brand is something that ideally makes you happy to go to work.

Remember, to stand out, find out what you stand for. I stand for helping people. As I mentioned earlier, my personal mission is: "I help people experience enthusiasm, love and wisdom to fulfill big dreams." So I am joyful as I write these words. I'm glad to support you as you step forward and make substantial progress on your goals.

The successful people I have interviewed who fulfill their goals also demonstrate skill in making their personal brand vivid and memorable. So how does this personal branding process work?

Author Bill Cates emphasizes these questions:
1. If I ran into great prospects for your business, how would I know it and how would you like me to introduce them to you?
2. If I were to introduce someone to you, whom I know you'd like to meet, what one sentence would I use to describe you and the way you do business?
3. What do I need to know about you and your business so that when I'm talking to people, I will know if you should meet them?
These are powerful questions.

As an example, I'll share with you one of my own answers that demonstrates my personal brand and that relates to the above questions.

When someone asks me (in an email message) about who my potential clients are, I reply:

"You could tell the person: 'Through his books, coaching and workshops on *10 Seconds to Wealth* and *Unleash Your Secret Charisma*, Tom Marcoux helps you communicate so powerfully and so easily that people naturally follow your lead. He helps you get the promotion, gain more customers—and rise to the next level of success and fulfillment.'"

* * *

I invite you to get to work on how you express your personal brand. It's like opening the door to your next opportunities. Think of your personal brand in this light: How are people going to hear your music if you don't blow your own horn?

Develop your own answers to the above powerful questions. And remember the essence of your personal brand is your answer to this significant question: *What are you best known for?*

Some Thoughts about "You Can Stand Out, Express Your Personal Brand, and Welcome Success"—and Negotiation

How can your personal brand help you in negotiations? If you effectively express your personal brand, it can serve as a powerful reputation that precedes you before you walk up to the negotiation table.

One powerful way to express your personal brand is to do some public speaking. Then, part of your personal brand will be "expert" and "highly competent person."

Over the years, I have trained thousands of students in powerful methods of public speaking. If you pause for a moment, you'll realize that "all speaking is public." That is, you have an audience—whether it is one, one hundred or one thousand.

Now, I'll share a special report that includes some of my best methods about public speaking which relate to you exerting personal power. Negotiation requires that you communicate effectively. See if you can discern how the following methods could apply to a negotiation. (Hint: giving a speech is a "form of dialogue" and negotiating is also a dialogue.)

* * * Beginning of Special Report * * *

**9 Deadly Mistakes to Avoid for Your Next Speech
by Tom Marcoux,
   America's Communication Coach**

This special report, just for you, is in three parts:

**PART I:
3 Big Mistakes to Avoid for Your Next Speech – How to Get Confident**

What is a springboard for your career success? Your ability to speak up in a meeting or to give a presentation.

Here are three big mistakes to avoid when giving your next speech:

Mistake #1: Letting fear and nervousness cripple you.

Does making a speech scare you? That's natural. It proves you're awake and thinking. Why? Because a poor speech could truly slow down your career.

Oh no. Now you're feeling the fear more. Good.

Good? Yes. Transform that fear into energy. Energy to prepare.

We have the power to transform fear into energy.

I remember a stunt I did in college. I thought, "Hey, I could jump up, grab that second floor balcony, and pull myself up." (Give me a break. I was young and stupid.)

Half way into pulling myself up, I realized that I was running out of energy. I could easily picture it: If I let go, I could fall, slip, and bash my head in. I could end up crippled. Then I got mad! I wasn't going to let one stupid action end my dreams. I exclaimed a particular curse word (no, I won't repeat it here) and pulled myself up. Yes, one word helped me focus my energy. At other times, I have helped clients use words like "I can do this!" to shift into an empowered state of being.

My point is that we all have the power to transform fear into energy. (And I hope you avoid goofy stunts.)

The big mistake that comes with letting fear and nervousness cripple you is that they may stop you from rehearsing. (Rehearsing is important for a speech or a stunt.)

How does fear stop us? What do we do when something hurts? We often run from it.

How do you run from it? You procrastinate. On some level, likely subconscious, you put thinking about your speech out of your mind. I'm not talking about worrying. Worrying can be a useless (and hurtful) way of recycling scared thoughts around and around.

Instead, any time you're feeling fear about giving a speech, find a small way to rehearse.

Action #1: Rehearse — even just a bit.

You can:
- Call a friend to ask if they can devote two minutes to listening to you rehearse the opening of your speech.
- Call your answering machine and record a two-minute rehearsal of your speech.
- Pick five friends and ask them to listen to five small sections of your speech.

To handle fear when you're in a meeting, write down some notes. Then raise your hand and speak up and refer to your notes. I emphasize to my clients: "If you don't speak up when you're in a meeting, even to ask a question, then you're invisible. You might as well stay home." (I have needed to remind myself of this detail when in faculty meetings.)

Now we move on to the next mistake . . .

Mistake #2: Getting embarrassed about making a mistake.

This one could stop us from even accepting an opportunity to make a career-skyrocketing speech. Have you, some years ago, given a speech and felt embarrassed? Did the audience laugh at you and not with you?

Terrible experience. Pain. Agony. Many of us will just duck and cover — and avoid speaking up in meetings or giving a presentation.

But this is not for you. You're going to seize opportunities to shine in your career. How? You learn *Recovery Methods*. These techniques are the first things that I teach my clients and my graduate students in my professional presentation class. You see, you don't have to fear making a mistake when you know how to recover from mistakes.

Here I will share two *Recovery Methods.*

- Say: "That's not what I meant to say. What I meant to say was _____."
- If your mind goes blank, ask a question or say: "Now, I want to emphasize . . ."

If your mind goes blank, take a breath. Please know that your audience probably welcomes a pause so they can catch up with their own thinking and the processing of your comments. Realize that they're hearing your material for the first time.

You could ask a question like: "We've covered a lot of material so far. What detail has connected with you?"

Or you could say: "Now, I want to emphasize . . ." What will you emphasize? Go back to the title of your speech. When I speak on "Power Time Management: More Time, Less Stress and Zero Procrastination," I often say, "What I want to emphasize is: We need something better than time management. Just because you write something on a To-Do list doesn't mean you'll get it done. What you need is Time-Leverage."

So let's remember:

Action #2: Practice Recovery Methods.

Here's the next mistake to avoid.

Mistake #3: Leaving out stories.

Want to persuade someone?

Good -- then learn to deal with resistance.

How do you avoid resistance altogether? Tell a story.

What captures attention better — a dry statistic or a story?

"When I held onto the hood of the speeding truck by my fingertips, I wasn't thinking about moving at 57 miles an hour or the cameraman getting the shot. I was focused on . . ."

Do I have your attention?

By the way, this points to another important detail about stories: It helps when it's your own true story. It's true that I hung onto the hood of a racing truck as a stunt in a feature film. (And, no, I wouldn't do it again.)

To my clients and graduate students, I emphasize that when you're telling a personal story, you are the expert of your own story. This is important. If you repeat a tired, old, clichéd story about someone else, you're treading on thin ice. What if you get a detail wrong? What if you turn the audience off like a light switch? For example, since I read many books a year, you can imagine how tired I am of reading that Thomas Edison said, "No, I didn't fail. I successfully found 5,000 ways the light bulb doesn't work." (By the way, that comment is not even accurate.)

Action #3: Share true personal stories and engage the audience (and avoid resistance).

Your true personal story gives the audience an experience. Make a point and attach a story.

* * *

So, let's be aware of the three mistakes:
Mistake #1: Letting fear and nervousness cripple you.
Mistake #2: Getting embarrassed about making a mistake.
Mistake #3: Leaving out stories.

Remember these methods:
Action #1: Rehearse — even just a bit.
Action #2: Practice Recovery Methods.
Action #3: Share true personal stories and engage the audience (and avoid resistance).

Researchers have noted that people on the fast track of success have one thing in common: They are good communicators.

How do you improve your skills? Get coaching and

rehearse. In this way, you condition yourself to do well in a trying situation. You'll find that this pays off again and again.

PART II:
Make Your Body Language Match Your Words — or Crash and Burn

Does your body language show your confidence?

Ever attend a speech and something was off? I mean, way off.

The speaker says the right words, although you really don't like him! It's likely that the speaker's body language and words contradict one another. Let's face it together. We like things that match and feel true.

For example, I have a friend who creates music like Mozart. When she listens to the first draft of the music I composed, her head bobs up and down in time with the beat. If she hears something that is a bit off, her head reflexively shakes "no." (Oh, give me a break. It's a rough draft. How her "no" move feels to me like a dismissal! But I digress.)

And that's what happens when your body language fails to match your words. Inside, the audience shakes with, "No . . . this is not truthful . . . I don't like this."
Now, I'll share 3 Big Mistakes and how you can take action to really connect with an audience (or in a meeting).

Mistake #1: Your words say you're confident and that your

product will help. But your body language says, "Don't hurt me."

Imagine you hear someone say, "I'm confident that my product will solve your problem." But the person is wringing his hands. Do you believe him?

Avoid "petting your own hand like a pet cat"
Often, when nervous, people pet one hand with the other hand. This looks like you're comforting yourself. It's as if you're saying to yourself, "There. There. I know you're nervous in front of the big, scary people."

Avoid the "Fig Leaf"
Another behavior to avoid is placing your hands together as if you're covering or protecting yourself near the bottom of your torso. This says, "I have no confidence."

Avoid the "Mr. Spock"
Mr. Spock often held his hands behind his back. It's almost as if he was saying, "I'd hit you, Captain, but my hands are clasped back here." (For non-"Star Trek" enthusiasts: Mr. Spock has emotions. He just restrains them.)

Action #1: Use your peripheral vision, notice your hands, and gently undo nervous behavior.

So, when you notice that your hands are doing something that reveals nervousness, just slowly and gently change your hand position. Avoid moving your hands in a way that says, "Oh! I did it again!" Just slowly move them.

Mistake #2: You try to answer a tough question, but your

body language says, "I'm lying" or "I'm scared" or "I'm incompetent."

Let's say a speaker answers, "Thanks for your question." But somehow you feel that she doesn't care, or that she doesn't like your question, or she doesn't like you!
How do you get this feeling? It is likely that only her face is pointed toward you.

It is reported that the FBI assesses whether a person is telling the truth by looking first at their feet, then hands and then their face. Why is the face the last considered? Because many of us have been conditioned by parents to control our face. You've probably heard a parent tell a child, "Get that look off your face!"

Action #2: Heart faces heart.
When you answer a question (even a tough question), turn your whole body and face the person. If appropriate, take one or two steps toward the person and include his or her name. Turn your body so heart faces heart and say, "Thanks, Sarah. I'm glad you brought that up. Now, I can mention . . ." But only try this if you can do it with sincerity.

Mistake #3: You try to hide your real thoughts and feelings, but your body language "stutters."

Ever hide your feelings? (Am I kidding?) Sure, we all do.

When we make a speech, our body language is speaking so loud that our words are often drowned out.

The solution? Find something you believe in to include in

your speech. How? Even in a dry, statistics-driven speech, find a way to include a true personal story. Your body language will line up with your words because you're saying something true and personal.

I learned this during my training as an actor and working as a feature film director. Often you'll see an actor start to slam a fist on the table—but there is a "stuttering" in his movement. Why? Because it is not true. The actor merely remembers the stage direction to slam his fist on the table. It would have better if he started out by saying something true to himself so his body language could flow naturally. The same method will work for you as a presenter.

Action #3: Find a chance to tell a true personal story so that your body language expresses naturalness and truth.
How can you attach a personal story when you are just conveying a statistic? You can relate your experience of how you responded upon first hearing that particular statistic.

* * *

Remember to avoid these mistakes related to body language:
Mistake #1: Your words say you're confident and that your product will help. But your body language says, "Don't hurt me."
Mistake #2: You try to answer a tough question, but your body language says, "I'm lying" or "I'm scared" or "I'm incompetent."
Mistake #3: You try to hide your real thoughts and feelings — but your body language "stutters."

Practice these positive actions:

Action #1: Use your peripheral vision, notice your hands, and gently undo nervous behavior.
Action #2: Heart faces heart.
Action #3: Find a chance to tell a true personal story so that your body language expresses naturalness and truth.

I'm glad to provide this information to you because your next speech can either catapult your career or give you a career-scar. (And if you're interested in one-to-one coaching, please contact my office at tomsupercoach@gmail.com).

Every moment you put into preparing your speech delivers a mountain of benefits.
Remember: *Courage is easier when you're prepared.*

PART III:
Mistakes that Bore Audiences and Embarrass You Instead, Get Them to Applaud and Say "Wow"!

Ever been terrified that you might embarrass yourself while you give a speech?

My first major speech, over 156 people in the audience, and SNORE! was the sound rising from the center of the crowd. A man snored like someone sawing wood.
I could have thrown up.

So let's talk about feeling embarrassed. It was embarrassing to feel that I was so boring that I couldn't keep somebody awake! (This was 20 years ago, people!)

You've felt embarrassed at some point—right? And you want strategies to avoid feeling embarrassed—yes? You're in the right place.

I began life as a young boy so shy that my leg fluttered like a hummingbird's wing. Later, as a professional speaker, I made some big mistakes. For example, 20 minutes into giving a speech to employees at a major Silicon Valley company, my assistant began frantically waving and gesturing, "Zip up! Zip up!" Yes—my fly was down. I nodded to stop her frantic waving.

I said, "I've just received some important news." I turned around, went out the back door and zipped up.

I returned and said, "For those of you who know what just happened—okay. For those of you who don't know what happened—good!"

Huge laughter flowed from the audience. The longest and loudest laughter of my career so far.

Why am I telling you this? To show you how I turned around the situation and made it fun for the audience. That's part of my "how are you doing" focus that I will explain below. The speech was not about me; it was about serving the audience.

Now we'll learn how to avoid feeling embarrassed.

Mistake #1: Thinking the speech is about you and that you will impress the audience.

Perhaps you noticed this phenomenon? We want something, but we ask for something else. The truth is, as a human being, we need connection. But we ask for approval. With an audience, we need connection but we try to impress the audience.

How can you avoid feeling embarrassed? It starts with your approach to the whole process of preparing a speech and then giving the speech. You notice the word "giving."

I guide my graduate students to do this exercise: Form two lines and stand 10 feet apart from your partner. Students on the left side of the room hold up a pen and say, "This is a pen. And this is for you." Then they walk over to their exercise partner and give him or her the pen.

In this way, each student experiences giving the pen (like giving a speech or an idea) to another person.

This is a big transition from: How am I doing (panic), to, how are you doing—and here's a gift (strength and purpose).

How do you avoid feeling embarrassed? You shift your thinking. I'll give you an example. I can get myself to feel embarrassed in an instant. All I need to do is recall dancing at a party when I was 15 years old. I didn't know how to dance. I remember dancing with a pretty girl—no, make that a stunning girl—and I was feeling supernaturally good. What did I do? I was feeling so light-hearted that I did a leaping kick at the balloon above my head. Ugh. I cringe even now. But—zap! In this present moment, I shift my thoughts to "I was so full of life!" (I don't even want to talk to you about when I did the backward roll on the floor.)

As I reframe the situation, I consider that being full of life is a good thing. As you can see, with a simple shift in my thoughts, I made the thought and feeling of embarrassment quiet down!

Solution #1: Shift your thoughts from "How am I doing" to "How are YOU doing? How may I serve YOU?"

The name of the game is to get into this present moment and connect with someone in the audience. If you make a mistake and feel embarrassed, immediately connect with an audience member. Find a way to lightly acknowledge the error, if appropriate. If you mispronounce a word, you could say, "Oh, don't use that word everyday." And then immediately ask a question like, "So, we've covered a lot of material so far. Is there something you'd like for me to clarify?"

People easily become impressed with you when you listen and show them that you are impressed with them!

Mistake #2: Read the speech.

An audience member at a conference says to herself, "Oh, no! She's going to read the speech. Gawd! How long will this last?!" Why is it boring when you read a speech? Because there's no connection.

Have you attended a live performance or a live play? Did you feel the "electricity"?

Did you notice something? I asked you some questions. Even through the printed word I was able to reach out to you and you responded to my questions. (Didn't you?)

A speaker who looks down to read has just severed any

connection with the audience.

Solution #2: Use notes in a way that works for you.

You can place your notes in unlikely places, like a side table instead of the lectern. Make sure that the notes are printed in large letters. Glance at the notes out of the corner of your eye. Be subtle.

Another way to handle notes is to place them on a posted note that you keep subtly in your hand. Just include the main ideas. Or you can write your notes on 3 x 5 cards that are attached with a metal ring. (In case you sneeze, the notes won't fall all over the stage).

The point is to glance at your notes only when you need to. It's okay to read a particular statistic. But then bring your eyes back to the audience. You are giving to them a gift of your thoughts and ideas.

Mistake #3: Talk at the audience.

"Man, this guy is full of himself. He thinks he is God's gift to us. He's wrong," an audience member thinks during a formal speech. If you don't enter into a "dialogue" with the audience, they'll default to feeling that you are talking at them. The audience may have a flashback to the feelings they experienced when authoritative parents talked at them.

When do people feel comfortable with us? When they know we value them — their ideas, their experience and their insights. How can you do that? Ask them a few questions. Listen. Express appreciation for good ideas. Repeat the ideas in this manner: "Thanks, Sarah, for the idea about ____. I'm glad that you brought that up. This idea helps us to now ____."

Be in the moment.

I always remember this quote: *"We must be willing to relinquish the life we've planned, so as to have the life that is waiting for us." – Joseph Campbell*

Similarly, you need to be willing to be in the moment and respond to the audience. Watch their faces. Observe their body language. Flow, respond, listen, serve.

Solution #3: Talk with the audience. Ask questions, listen and respond.

For some speeches, it's better that you don't ask the audience for questions or answers. In this case you can still pose rhetorical questions like: "Ever hesitate to call a prospective customer?" Then pause and let people remember. After a moment, you can smile and say, "I can see your faces. Many of you are nodding. And yes, I've been in the same situation. Here's what we can do . . ."

In this way, you have begun a dialogue with your audience. You have established a connection. Good for you.

* * * * *

Remember to avoid these mistakes:
Mistake #1: Thinking the speech is about you and that you will impress the audience.

Mistake #2: Read the speech.
Mistake #3: Talk at the audience.

Apply these solutions:
Solution #1: Shift your thoughts from "How am I doing" to "How are YOU doing? How may I serve YOU?"
Solution #2: Use notes in a way that works for you.
Solution #3: Talk with the audience. Ask questions, listen and respond.

Rehearse these effective methods. You'll be glad that you did.

* * * END OF ABOVE SPECIAL REPORT * * *

One of the reasons that I shared the above special report about effective public speaking is that negotiation takes as much, if not more, preparation as giving a speech. **Additionally, if the person you will negotiate with has seen you give an effective speech, you have the status of "expert," and this is good leverage to have when you begin a negotiation.**

9) TIRED OF FEELING STUCK? HOW TO RELEASE YOURSELF TO A BETTER LIFE

Ever heard a friend say, "I hate this!"?
That's a lot of energy going into the "hate" direction. And it's a waste.
It would be helpful to shift the direction of that energy. How? Use the following powerful words:

- Flexible
- Listening
- Open to coaching

These words open the door to new ideas and new possibilities. I recall Bill Gates comment: "Success is a lousy teacher. It seduces smart people into thinking they can't lose." If you think you can't lose, you're unlikely to seek coaching.

You can gain coaching in many ways. Here are few ways in which I gain coaching:

- I bring my new ideas to a small circle of trusted friends and advisors and hear their insights.
- I have a coach.
- I participate in a monthly phone conference with fellow members of my Breakthrough Mastermind Group. During the phone call, we coach each other.
- I study books by high achieving people every day.
- I listen to audio programs by high achievers.
- I hire book editors, graphic artists, video editors, tax planning personnel, attorneys and medical personnel as needed. I learn from all of the professionals that I hire. I ask them questions as we go along.

Unfortunately, a number of people have avoided the positive habit of gaining coaching and insight from others. Ever sit with friends and one friend talks about a problem? The other friends offer solutions but your dispirited friend says, "No. That won't work." "No, I tried that." "No." It almost seems that the person prefers to be stuck.

A number of my graduate students are hoping to find a

mentor.

I share with them an example of the process:

a) At a networking event, a young person, "Mira," asks a question of a top person in an industry.

b) Mira takes action based on the advice she received.

c) Mira reports back (via a phone call or an email) to the potential mentor.

d) At this point, the potential mentor may offer additional advice.

Here's an important point: Regardless of how the result turned out, report back to the potential mentor. The potential mentor will likely be glad to hear that someone did something with her advice. And here's the great part: she will likely offer some refinement on her original advice. She might even say, "Oh. You can talk with my Cousin Hyrum about that. Here's his email address."

So if you find yourself saying, "I hate this!" consider asking yourself:

- How can I be flexible here?
- Who knows more about this than I do? How can I ask the person questions?
- Has someone offered a possible helpful idea? Was I shut down? Can I take an appropriate action?

If you feel stuck, something must change—your actions, attitude or strategy.

As I mentioned earlier, one empowering idea I have come across is "this is an AND universe—not an OR universe."

For example, I know a number of people who work at a job to earn rent money, AND they pursue their artwork, achieving some progress each day.

Do something new.

Take a small step. It will be better than zero. That is, it will be an improvement over no action and not even a small benefit.

You don't have to do something in a perfect way. For example, years ago, I wrote a book entitled *Communicate to Win*. I didn't find that title to truly express the essence of what I do.

Recently, the third edition is retitled: *Be Heard and Be Trusted*. Now, that felt better to me. I felt my heart warm up and a big smile graced my face.

Take a step forward—that's where the fun and delightful surprises are.

Some Thoughts on "Tired of Feeling Stuck" and Negotiation

One of the fastest ways to get unstuck is to engage a coach. Before a tough negotiation, it can really help to have a session with a coach who specializes in helping people prepare before a negotiation. (For example, I coach people in person and over the phone.)

When we're stuck, we're usually cycling the same tired perceptions and thoughts—over and over. We need new input. The power of coaching is that the skilled coach will ask you focused questions customized in the moment to help you uncover your hidden desires and strengths.

Coaches can also help you stay accountable. One author

wrote: "A goal is accountable when it's countable."

Get new input. Unleash your energy so you'll be at your best during a negotiation and beyond.

10) NEED SOME RELIEF? BRING HUMOR AND LAUGHTER INTO YOUR LIFE

The pressure was too much. Susan thought she'd break. She tried to talk it out. She told the truth to a friend, "I'm furious. It's not fair. My roommates just abandoned me and went to a movie and left the mess to me. And the landlord was going to inspect our apartment the next morning."

But Susan didn't get any relief until . . . she laughed. How? She watched a brief TV show that she had prerecorded.

Susan is onto something here. In fact, I watch something funny and I laugh every day. One of my favorite shows is *Whose Line Is It, Anyway?* This is a show in which a number of comedians improvise comedic skits.

For many of us, just some brief laughter brings genuine relief. We feel better. The world seems less oppressive. Somehow, an inner lightness arises. The facts of the situation may not change, but somehow, we have awakened our inner resources.

When I teach graduate students how to add humor to their speeches, I share these details:
1. Humor always has a target.
2. You are the safe target for your humor.

3. Humor happens with the last word in the sentence.

4. Tell a story (if expressing a joke doesn't flow easily for you).

5. Humor involves "pain at a distance."

Recently, I visited my mother. Talking with her can be a challenge because she is somewhat reserved and she does not say much. I remembered the principle: "Tell a story." So I started telling a story and I discovered the humor in the story. What a joy to see my mother laughing. I glanced to my right and saw that my sweetheart chuckled, too.

As a teenager, when I completed an internship, a kind co-worker gave me a gift. She included a note: "Be the rose that perfumes the hand that crushes it." At the time, I didn't quite connect with that phrase.

I have an optimistic approach to life. I can now connect to part of the spirit of the co-worker's note. Now, I say, "Learn to inspire laughter in others. Their laughter splashes onto you." No towel needed.

Some Thoughts on "Relief and Humor"—and Negotiation

Appropriate humor can have a place in negotiation. Before the serious talk, it helps to connect with people on a human level. You need to be careful with humor. It's best to use yourself as the target. *Warning:* do not overdo self-deprecating humor because it can backfire. With too much self-deprecation, you can actually decrease your positive feelings about yourself. Too much self-deprecation could also make you appear weak to the other person.

Sometimes, it can help to share a couple of humorous details. If you know the other person has a cat, you could share a humorous story—if you have a cat. Some people are "dog people" so pay attention and don't lose them with an overlong cat story.

People often connect when talking about their children. Parenthood is often cited as both a journey of joy and some of the toughest times to endure. If you're in someone's office, you can connect about something you see: a photo, an award, or something else.

For example, I once saw photos of fish in a bank vice-president's office. I asked, "Did you take those photos?" With a big smile, he said, "Yes!" Great! An instant connection.

If I'm in someone's office and she has a photo that features her yacht, I might share the story of the time I hung off the side of a small yacht to film a particular shot for a movie. When we hit choppy water, I yelled, "Turn the boat around! Turn the boat around!"

11) FEEL YOU HAVE NO TIME? HERE'S WHAT YOU CAN DO

Imagine a time when you're running fast—from appointment to appointment, errand to errand. Work is slamming you hard with overtime. You can barely catch your breath. And you're not sleeping much. Ugh. Pain.

There must be some relief possible. Yes. And, here's a

helpful idea: "Better than zero." I use this phrase as a reminder that I can do something, perhaps, something small, but it will result in better outcomes than doing nothing.

Do you feel that you don't have time for exercise? Just recently, my sweetheart and I visited another city and stayed at a friend's home. I got my exercise in by suggesting that we all take a walk.

Now there are some people who scoff at a walk instead of running or hitting the gym. And to that I reply: "Better than zero."

And there are a number of days when I apply the "Power of 10" (10 pushups, 10 sit-ups, 10 palm strikes, 10 side kicks and so forth). It just takes a few minutes.

How about expressing your love to your romantic partner? Pick up a card while you're getting groceries. No time to get the perfect card? Pick a good card and write endearments to augment the message printed in the card. Don't have the words? How about reminding your loved one of good moments shared on a vacation and say: "Thank you. I treasure those moments with you. I love you."
I always remember this quote:

"We do not remember days, we remember moments." – *Cesare Pavese*

Make the most of your moments.

Some Thoughts on Feeling You Have No Time—and Negotiation

Sometimes, I get surprised. I'll hear a client say that he has no time to prepare. But he's not seeing the whole picture. If you don't prepare for the negotiation, you'll find yourself losing double or triple the amount of time trying to undo the damage that poor results of negotiation bring. Devote even just nine minutes a day to preparation (over a few days) and you save a lot of time and effort later. Devoting nine minutes a day also keeps your subconscious mind working for the improvement of your upcoming negotiation.

* * *

Earlier, I mentioned how preparation for giving a speech and preparation for negotiation are similar. Both require thinking carefully through your points. Both also require rehearsal. You can even prepare for negotiating by accepting opportunities for public speaking. (A number of people feel the same nervousness before a speech that one feels before a crucial negotiation, and public speaking gives you the opportunity to become adept at doing well even when feeling somewhat nervous.)

12) HOW YOU CAN RADIATE CHARISMA WITH YOU NEXT SPEECH

Would you love to give a speech that moves an audience?

Would you also love to feel better as you're preparing a speech and while giving it?

You can. *[By the way, it is a great advantage before you enter a negotiation for you to be perceived as an expert, and a good speech helps create that perception.]* I help my own clients and graduate students go from cowering to compelling. One of my graduate students used my methods and she won the coveted Charles Schwab scholarship for her presentation.

You can become as charismatic in front of an audience as she was. To be charismatic, my clients learn to express "the 3 Cs": Caring, Concerned and Competent.

Although I'm an excellent public speaker now, that wasn't always the case. As a shy boy, playing the piano for a group of seniors at a retirement home, I was terrified. My leg shook so badly I was afraid my foot would fall off the sustain pedal with a big thud. My attention was on "How am I doing?"

Through years of training and public speaking, I learned to shift from "How am I doing?" to "How are you doing?"

A charismatic person makes you feel like you're the most important person in the room. The person makes you feel so good that you naturally want to listen and cooperate with him or her.

To express the traits "Caring and Concerned," be sure to ask gentle questions and listen. One gentle question I ask is: "When you first heard about this presentation, what were you hoping or expecting that I'd talk about?" I continue by asking, "What specific situation would you like me to address so you can return to your desk and feel that you got exactly what you needed from this presentation? I'll write down your questions here (on a white board)." In this way, my speech is never canned and I discover what the audience is specifically concerned about.

Similarly, to be charismatic, your message is: "How are you doing? How can I help you meet your goals?"

The truth is, as a human being, we need connection. But we ask for approval. With an audience, we need connection but instead we try to impress the audience.

We do this because we are afraid that if we don't impress the audience, we will be embarrassed. How can you avoid feeling embarrassed? It starts with your approach to the whole process of preparing a speech and then giving it. Take note that I said "giving."

To help my graduate students better understand the concept of giving during class, I guide them in this exercise: I have them form two lines, standing 10 feet apart. Students on the left side of the room hold up a pen and say, "This is a pen. And this is for you." Then they walk over to the person opposite them and give him or her the pen.

In this way, each student experiences giving the pen (like giving a speech or an idea) to another person.

This is a big transition from: How am I doing (panic), to, how are you doing—and here's a gift (strength and purpose).

For the "Competent," component of the three C's you'll do well by dropping distracting behaviors that scream "nervous person here." Here are ways to help you appear calm.

1) Use belly-breathing. To calm yourself, you can place your hand on your belly. Breathe in through your nose and have your belly expand. Hold the breath for a moment. Then breathe out through your mouth. You can tell yourself "relax." You can also affirm: "I'll listen to them; they'll have a good time." Do this before you walk on stage.

2) Get your hands away from each other. I tell my graduate students, "Don't pet the cat," meaning sometimes people comfort themselves by petting one hand with the other—as if one hand was a cat. This behavior reeks of fear.

3) Use gestures to "take up more space." I learned this detail from Lynda Obst (producer of *Sleepless in Seattle* and *Contact*). She is small in stature. So she talks about needing to "take up more space."

Rehearse standing up tall with shoulders back. Gesture in a comfortable and "open" manner, that is, with your palms up and away from your body.

4) Walk and plant. This is a prime behavior of "owning the room." Walk a few steps and then "plant your feet" that is, stand still and deliver a paragraph. Then walk a few steps to another part of the audience and then plant your feet again.

5) Heart faces heart. Do you want to show that you're confident? Turn to an audience member who asks a question. When you face the person and take a step toward him or her, your heart faces the person's heart. You demonstrate that you're interested in the person. You also demonstrate that you're not afraid of the question.

To radiate charisma, it really helps to rehearse—even just nine minutes a day. Rehearse in front of people. You can rehearse by calling up a friend with your cell phone and going through the first two minutes of your speech.

Before closing, I want to share three vital principles from the third edition of my book *Be Heard and Be Trusted:*

1) We don't need you to be perfect; we do need you to be genuine.
2) You can turn a question into gift, even if it was thrown like a spear.
3) You are the expert of your own story.

So, to be charismatic, demonstrate that you care about your audience. Share a personal story or two so you give the audience an experience.

Charisma is not about impressing people, by trying to convince them how great you are.

It's about encouraging people and helping them unleash how great they are.

They'll love you for it!

Some Thoughts about Giving a Great Speech—and Negotiation

It's best when you're meeting new people to have them experience you as a speaker at an event. Why? You come across as an expert. Your perceived competence and power are enhanced.

Picture this. You happen to meet a prospective client

while you both sit in the audience of a speech given at an association meeting. You might meet on the level of peers. But if you gave the speech, you would literally be a "step up"—having given a speech from the stage.

It's truly valuable to be perceived as an expert. By the way, if you have any hesitancy about identifying yourself as an expert, here is a useful insight. I developed a phrase after reading some paragraphs written by the author Bob Bly. He described what he does to be an expert. I boiled down some of his phrases to this short phrase: "An expert has a system that people like and use."

When you give a speech or presentation, demonstrate how people have liked and have used the methods you're suggesting. You'll be perceived as an expert and your ability to command respect and attention during a negotiation is enhanced.

A FINAL WORD AND THE SPRINGBOARD TO YOUR DREAMS

Congratulations on your efforts with this book.

We have worked with countermeasures to protect your from the darkest methods of negotiation masters.

I'm grateful for this opportunity to provide these insights so you can leap forward to making your dreams come true.

For more training, consider getting the *Home Study Course of Darkest Secrets of Persuasion and Seduction Masters: How to Protect Yourself and Turn the Power to Good.*

Meanwhile, please return to these pages and practice the various methods so that you continue to become stronger and you continue to protect yourself from the darkest secrets of persuasion and seduction masters.

You now know how to turn the power to good.

Please consider gaining special training through my coaching (phone and in-person), workshops and presentations.

Note the other eight books in this series. . .

- Darkest Secrets of Charisma
- Darkest Secrets of Persuasion and Seduction Masters: How to Protect Yourself and Turn the Power to Good
- Darkest Secrets of Making a Pitch to the Film and Television Industry
- Darkest Secrets of Business Communication: Using Your Personal Brand
- Darkest Secrets of Small Business Marketing
- Darkest Secrets of Spiritual Seduction Masters
- Darkest Secrets of the Film and Television Industry Every Actor Should Know
- Darkest Secrets of Film Directing

See my blog at
www.BeHeardandBeTrusted.com

The best to you,
Tom
Tom Marcoux,
America's Communication Coach
P.S. View the 8 Other *Darkest Secrets* books:
See **Free Chapters** of Tom Marcoux's 19 books
at http://amzn.to/ZiCTRj

Titles include:
Be Heard and Be Trusted
Nothing Can Stop You This Year
Truth No One Will Tell You
10 Seconds to Wealth
Your Secret Charisma
Wake Up Your Spirit to Prosperity
The Cat Advantage
— and more.

(For coaching, reach Tom Marcoux
at tomsupercoach@gmail.com)

Tom Marcoux

EXCERPT FROM
DARKEST SECRETS OF PERSUASION AND SEDUCTION MASTERS: HOW TO PROTECT YOURSELF AND TURN THE POWER TO GOOD

by Tom Marcoux

BOOK I
Darkest Secrets of Persuasion Masters

I never expected to write *Darkest Secrets of Persuasion and Seduction Masters: How to Protect Yourself and Turn the Power to Good.*

But I was angry and I had to stand up for you.

When I was a child, I was hurt badly. My parents could not protect me. As a young man, in one of my first business deals, I was hurt terribly.

Now, I am in my 40's, with gray in my hair, and for 27

years I have been taking action to protect people.

And now is the time for me to protect you with the Countermeasures I reveal in this book.

Every human being needs to be able to
break the trance that a Manipulator
creates. You need to make good decisions
so you are safe and you keep growing
—and you are not cut down and crippled.

This Darkest Secrets material is so intense that I first released it only with the counterbalance of my most energizing and uplifting books, *Nothing Can Stop You This Year!* and *10 Seconds to Wealth: Master the Moment Using Your Divine Gifts.*

An interviewer asked me: "Who can be the Manipulator?"

A co-worker, a boss, a salesperson, someone you're dating, and someone you think is a friend.

Now is the time—this very minute—for me to write this book to protect you.

I must speak the truth.

These darkest secrets of "persuasion masters" are …

Wait a minute! Let's say it plainly: These are the darkest secrets of masters of manipulation. Throughout this book, I will call these people what they are: Manipulators.

Dictionary.com defines "manipulate" as "To influence or manage shrewdly or deviously…. To tamper with or falsify for personal gain."

In this book, we will look on a manipulator as one who deviously influences someone with no concern about that person's well-being, and who causes harm to that person.

Here is the first Darkest Secret:

Darkest Secret #1:
Manipulators Make You Hurt
and Then Offer the Salve.

Manipulators would invite you to go out in the sun for hours and then sell you the salve to soothe your burns. The problem is that we don't notice that this is what they're doing.

For example, you're considering the purchase of a house. A Manipulator asks the question, "So, where would you put your TV?" This question is designed to put you into a trance.

Dictionary.com defines "trance" as "a half-conscious state, seemingly between sleeping and waking, in which ability to function voluntarily may be suspended." Let's condense this: in a trance you may not be able to function freely.

Here is the second Darkest Secret:

Darkest Secret #2:
Manipulators Put You into a Trance.

To protect yourself, you must learn to use *Countermeasures to Break the Trance.*

All the Countermeasures (actions you can take to break

the trance) in this book will make you stronger and more capable of protecting yourself.

Now, we'll view the third Darkest Secret:

Darkest Secret #3:
Manipulators Care Nothing for You and Human Decency: They'll lie, cheat, and do whatever they need to do so they win—but their charm masks all this.

Let's return to the example of a Manipulator selling you a house. A Manipulator does not pause for an instant to see if you can truly afford the new house. The Manipulator would neglect to mention that you will not only have your mortgage payment of $900. There will be additional costs: home repairs, property tax, water, electricity, homeowner's insurance, and more. The Manipulator only emphasizes what he or she knows you want to hear: "Look! $900 is better than the $1500 you're paying for rent, which is just going down the toilet. And the $900 is an investment."

Let's go back to **Darkest Secret #1:**
Manipulators make you hurt and then offer the salve.

The Manipulator has you feeling good about the solution (salve) and feeling bad about your current life situation.

How? A Manipulator will make you hurt through questions such as:

• What bothers you about paying $1500 a month for rent? (The Manipulator will use a derisive tone when he says the word rent.)

• What is not smart about paying rent on someone else's house instead of investing in your own house?

• How do you feel about your children walking in the neighborhood where you live now?

Do you see how these questions are designed to make you hurt enough so that you'll buy?

An interviewer asked me, "Tom, aren't these good arguments for purchasing a house?"

"What we're looking at is the intention of the influencer," I replied. "Let's look at our definition of a manipulator as one who deviously influences someone with no concern about that person's well-being, and who causes harm to that person. If the person truly cannot afford the house, he or she will be harmed by buying it. If the manipulator conceals the truth, the manipulator is doing harm. That's the important difference."

Some friends of mine are ethical and helpful real estate agents who truthfully reveal the whole situation and help the purchaser achieve her own goals.

In this book, we are talking about another type of person; that is, unethical Manipulators.

* * *

In any given moment, we need to remember the tactics Manipulators use. We will focus on the word D.A.R.K. so you can remember details easily and protect yourself from Manipulators.

D — Dangle something for nothing

A — Alert to scarcity

R — Reveal the Desperate Hot Button

K — Keep on pushing buttons

We'll begin with *Dangle something for nothing* with the next chapter.

CHAPTER TWO: DANGLE SOMETHING FOR NOTHING

The first method of D.A.R.K. is *Dangle Something for Nothing.*

What do conmen and conwomen do to seize your attention? They make you think you're getting a "steal."

I recently saw a documentary in which a conman on a street in England showed a toy that looked like it was dancing. This fake product was actually dancing because of a hidden, invisible thread. The conman was dangling something for nothing. The Entranced Buyer thought he was getting something worth $20 for only $5. That was the trick. The Entranced Buyer felt that he was getting $15 extra of value for his $5. What the Buyer really got was something worth nothing. Similarly, I know someone who purchased a copy of a Disney movie from a street vendor in San Francisco. She brought the copy home and it was unwatchable—and the street vendor was never seen again.

An old phrase goes, "A conman cannot con someone who is not looking for something for nothing."

How to Protect Yourself from "Dangle Something for Nothing"

Stop! Get on your cell phone and talk through the "deal" with someone you know who thinks clearly. Go home. Think about it. Do some research on the Internet. Listen to your gut feelings. If the salesman or conman is too insistent, get away from that Manipulator. Get quiet. Have a cup of water. Cool down. Break the Trance!

Break the Trance and Identify the Crucial Detail

Earlier, I mentioned that a Manipulator puts you into a trance. An added problem is that we put ourselves into a trance. For example, as you read this, are you thinking about your right toe? Most likely not (unless you stubbed your toe recently). The point is that we only focus on a tiny percentage of what is going on in our life.

Around fifteen years ago, I caused myself trouble because I put myself into a trance. I discovered that under certain conditions, friendship can make you nearly deaf. Here's how: I was producing a song for a motion picture. A good friend was singing backup in the chorus. Because of our friendship, I wanted him to sound great. I completely missed the Crucial Detail. In this kind of situation, the Crucial Detail is that what truly counts is how the lead singer sounds! I made a song that I could not release. What a waste of time and money! I had put myself into a trance.

In any situation in which the Manipulator is "dangling something for nothing," we often fall into a trance and miss the Crucial Detail. The most important detail is not that we're saving money if we order before midnight tonight. What counts is whether the product creates a lasting, crucial benefit in our lives. And is the benefit of the product worth the cost? Some people even program themselves to make mistakes by saying, "I can't pass up a bargain." The bargain is not the Crucial Detail.

Secrets to Break the Trance

This is the process of B.R.E.A.K.S. It will help you remember the proven methods to break a trance.

B — Breathe
R — Relax
E — Envision
A — Act on aromas
K — Keep moving
S — Smile

Secret #1: Breathe

Remember Darkest Secret #1: Manipulators make you hurt and then offer the salve. The Manipulator wants to put you into a state of being that fills you with a sense of urgency and anxiety. Oh, no! I'm going to miss the sale!

Stop this highly vulnerable state. Take a deep breath. Do it now. Take a deep breath and let your belly "get fat" by filling it with air. As you breathe out, let your belly deflate. Breathe in through your nose and breathe out through your mouth. This is called belly-breathing. Repeat the actions of belly-breathing three times. Good. Now, do you feel different? Remember, when you are relaxed, you are strong.

Secret #2: Relax

You become stronger when you condition yourself to relax in the face of adversity. Researchers note that when an

Olympic athlete is confronted with the most stressful moment in her life, she has prepared in advance. She has given herself ways to calm down. Two powerful methods are described in this section about B.R.E.A.K.S. One is breathing, and the other is envisioning.

A special part of relaxing is the effective use of your posture. Many of us think that we're relaxed when we slouch. However, I was taught by three physical therapists that when you sit up and align your vertebrae, you are more relaxed because your back's bone structure is naturally supporting you. Many of us discover that placing a pillow behind the lumbar-area of our back helps us sit up better. If you are sitting or standing when talking with a Manipulator, ensure that your posture is aligned. You will have more power to protect yourself.

Secret #3: Envision

Envision an image that makes you feel strong. Often, our strongest images come from movies that we saw when we were young. Some of my clients envision being strong like Xena the Warrior Princess or Superman. One client thinks of Sean Connery as James Bond. Immediately, this client walks smoothly with poise. He feels confident. Act as if you are, and you are!

Also, envision yourself being quite aware of your surroundings. On vacation, many of us become entranced by our new surroundings. Travelers let their guard down. A conperson catches them at a weak moment. It's important to stay in the present and be alert to what's going on. Stay present with your needs, and shop around before making a large purchase. Be prepared to walk away.

Watch out for Manipulators who are slick, fast talkers. They try to get your money, and just minutes after they succeed, you realize what happened.

But this is not for you! You can remind yourself with an internal comment: "I am aware. What is really going on here?"

Secret #4: Act on Aromas
Let's notice the power of an aroma.

Smell is a potent wizard that transports you
across thousands of miles
and all the years you have lived.
– Helen Keller

Nothing is more memorable than a smell.
One scent can be unexpected, momentary and fleeting,
yet conjure up a childhood summer
beside a lake in the mountains.
– Diane Ackerman

You need to be able to calm down within seconds. One of the fastest ways to do that is to use a favorite aroma. One of my clients has conditioned herself to calm down by smelling lavender. The process for her was to recline in a hot bath and smell lavender simultaneously. Now, the smell of lavender relaxes her limbs quickly.

Remember, when you are relaxed, you neutralize the Manipulator's tactic to make you feel that buying something now is an urgent matter. You let go of any anxious feelings the Manipulator seeks to create in you. Use an aroma to help you feel relaxed and strong.

Secret #5: Keep Moving

A trance often transfixes or freezes us, making us still. Sometimes, the most powerful way to break a trance is to use a movement that you prepared in advance. One of my clients closes his right fist and taps it on his right thigh. In his mind, he repeats the phrase: "I am my own person!" This helps him break out of a trance induced by a Manipulator.

Another client quietly snaps her fingers near her waist. This reminds her to "snap out of it."

Secret #6: Smile

Smile when you detect a Manipulator using a manipulation method. Why? If you get angry, you become vulnerable. Remember: Manipulators make you hurt and then offer the salve.

Often when we're angry, we don't realize that beneath the anger is fear. What fear? Fear of being taken advantage of. Become strong when you identify what makes you angry.

Pull out a sheet of paper or write in your personal journal. Write the headings of two columns.

a) What Makes Me Angry
b) What Fear Might Underlie My Anger

Write the two items next to each other.
Here is an example:
A clerk is rude to me. ===> I'm afraid that I'm worthless and not worthy of being treated with respect and kindness

The list above provides good information for you. When confronted with a Manipulator that pushes your fear buttons, you can say to yourself, "Oh! That touched my fear of losing an advantage. Okay, I feel this fear—but I am more than this fear. I am intelligent and capable."

You will feel better when you smile upon detecting a Manipulator's tactic. You will feel more in control. Researchers have shown that the act of smiling actually changes one's body chemistry. Get your body on your side.

Smile and break the trance-of-anxiety that the Manipulator attempts to use against you.

Point to Remember:
Manipulators dangle something for nothing.

Your Countermeasure:
Identify the Crucial Detail. Use these questions and statements:
• What benefit do I really want?
• Is this benefit worth the costs?
• Do I know all the costs?
• I will ask and ask until I am certain about the risks involved.
• Finally, I will contact someone I respect who is outside the area and run the situation past this trusted advisor.

CHAPTER 3: ALERT TO SCARCITY

The second method of D.A.R.K. is Alert to Scarcity

Have you ever been in a group situation and felt your

body shudder with discomfort? In several seminars, a seminar leader says, "Fifteen hundred people are here, and only 200 seats are available for the special event." Even before the seminar leader finishes his point, people are getting up and running to the back of the room to sign up for the event, which costs thousands of dollars. The seminar leader has told us that the situation is one of scarcity. There are not enough seats! One must take action immediately or lose out forever!

Wait a minute! How many of those people who get up immediately are plants? A plant is an actor or actress who fakes extraordinary interest in the product. (Side note: Did you know that the manager of a certain big-time singer in the 40s planted girls [actresses] in the audience to scream and swoon?) Also, conmen and conwomen use plants in the infamous shell game on a city street. The con-game includes shills (planted customers).

The point here is that a Manipulator creates the perception of scarcity to inspire a feeling of urgency in you. Why? Because we become afraid when we think we're going to lose something. "No! Don't take it away!"

How to Protect Yourself from "Alert to Scarcity"

Stop. Think. Will there truly never be another chance to get this information? What are the bad consequences of you over-extending and jacking up your credit card debts? Are there really only 200 seats available? Will this seminar leader go out of business so he won't be around to hold this special event again next year?

Pay attention! Do you feel a twinge of urgency? A raging

feeling of urgency? Breathe. Drink a glass of water. Talk with someone you trust. Pull out a piece of paper and write things down that answer the following questions:

Questions to Deal With Feelings of Urgency
1. What is this offer?
2. How do I feel?
3. Am I vulnerable now?
4. What am I afraid of losing?
5. Where else can I put this money? What would be good or better about that?
6. Does the seller care at all whether I get value from his product?
7. What technique is the seller using?
8. Is the product really in such short supply?
9. Have I considered other ways to get the product's benefits?
10. How might I be hurt if I go ahead with this purchase?
11. Do I know all the costs? Have I asked enough questions to get all the information I need?
12. Is the cost worth the benefits?
13. How can I be sure that I will even get those benefits?
14. How do I know if any of the salesperson's claims are true? Who told me that this offer actually provides the stated benefits?
15. Can I be sure that I can get my money back?
16. Is this offer worth my time? (My time is something I can never get back.)

When you write your answers down, you might surprise yourself. "Do I really think this? That doesn't make sense. Look! I've let this Manipulator make me scared of losing something."

An interviewer asked, "Don't many of us think things through quickly? I don't know if I would go through such a list of questions—or even remember them."

"If you're going to a seminar or an open house, bring a copy of your questions in your pocket. Then you will have the tools to be stronger," I replied.

Focus on Intuition versus Fear

Some of my clients have said, "But I had an intuition that I needed to attend that special event." This brings up a crucial distinction about our feelings and what may be true intuition.

Intuition includes feelings that help you stretch and grow.

Fear, on the other hand, includes feelings that make you contract and withdraw or hide to protect yourself.

The problem is that some of us allow certain fears to blind us so we don't take appropriate action. In the book, *The Gift of Fear*, author Gavin De Becker points out that we need to stay aware and listen to ourselves. For example, if a woman feels uneasy about entering an elevator with a particular man—she should honor her intuition in this matter and stay off that elevator. Unfortunately, some women discount their feelings of dread and tell themselves, "Oh, you're just being silly. You'll look stupid refusing to get on that elevator." Some of these individuals end up dead.

Here's the point. For years, I have been studying and writing about intuition. The way we can effectively work with our intuition is by making space for our intuition. We do this by sitting quietly with our feelings. We must seek to take more time with our intuition. We can do this by taking a piece of paper and pausing to answer questions, such as:

Questions that Help Your Intuition Speak Up
1. What can I gain here?
2. How would I grow from this experience?
3. Can I be hurt here?
4. Do the costs outweigh the benefits of this product/service?
5. Do I know all the costs?
6. What questions do I need to ask so I am well-informed?
7. Is the salesperson "playing" my fears?
8. What would it cost me if I missed this opportunity?
9. Is this really an opportunity?
10. How else can I gain benefits like these?
11. How can I create more space for my intuition?
12. How about if I say, "Let me sleep on it"?
13. Is this a situation for: If in doubt, leave it out?
14. Can I go to a positive friend (one not mired in the habits of fear) and get her intuitive feelings about the offer? I will note my feelings that come up when I hear her impressions.

End of Excerpt from
Darkest Secrets of Persuasion and Seduction Masters: How to Protect Yourself and Turn the Power to Good
Copyright 2013 Tom Marcoux Media, LLC

Purchase your copy of this book at
Amazon.com or BarnesandNoble.com
See **Free Chapters** of Tom Marcoux's 17 books
at http://amzn.to/ZiCTRj

ABOUT THE AUTHOR

Tom Marcoux helps people like you fulfill big dreams. Known as America's Communication Coach, Tom has authored 17 books with sales in 15 countries. One of his *Darkest Secrets* books rose to #1 on Amazon.com Hot New Releases in Business Life (and in Business Communication). He guides clients and audiences (IBM, Sun Microsystems, etc.) to success in job interviewing, public speaking, media relations, and branding. A member of the National Speakers Assoc., he is a professional coach and guest expert on TV, radio, and print, and was dubbed "the Personal Branding Instructor" by the *San Francisco Examiner.* Tom addressed National Assoc. of Broadcasters' Conference six years running. With a degree in psychology, Tom is a guest lecturer at **Stanford University**, DeAnza, & California State University, and teaches public speaking, science fiction cinema/literature and comparative religion at Academy of Art University. Winner of a special award at the Emmys, Tom wrote, directed, and produced a feature film that the distributor took to the Cannes film market, and the film gained international distribution. He is engaged in book/film projects *Crystal Pegasus* (children's) and *TimePulse* (science fiction). See TomSuperCoach.com and Tom's well-received blog at

www.BeHeardandBeTrusted.com

Tom Marcoux can help you with **speech writing** and **coaching for your best performance.**

As Tom says, *Make Your Speech a Pleasant Beach.*

Join Tom's Linkedin.com group: *Executive Public Speaking and Communication Power.*

Get a **Free** report: "9 Deadly Mistakes to Avoid for Your

Next Speech and 9 Surefire Methods" at
   http://tomsupercoach.com/freereport9Mistakes4Speech.ht
ml

Tom Marcoux has trained CEOs, small business owners,
and graduate students to speak with impact and gain
audiences' tremendous approval and cooperation. *Learn how
to present and get thunderous applause!*
"Tom, Thanks for your coaching and work with me on
revising my speech at a major university. Working with you
has been so enlightening for me. Through your gentle
prodding and guidance I was able to write a speech that
connects with the audience. I wish everyone could
experience the transformation I have undergone. You have
helped me discover the warm and compelling stories that
now make my speech reach hearts and uplift minds. This
was truly an empowering experience. I cannot thank you
enough for your great assistance." — J.S.

Become a fan of Tom's graphic novels/feature films:

Science fiction: *TimePulse*
www.facebook.com/timepulsegraphicnovel

Fantasy Thriller: *Jack AngelSword*
type "JackAngelSword" at Facebook.com

Children's Fantasy: *Crystal Pegasus*
www.facebook.com/crystalpegasusandrose

See **Free Chapters** of Tom Marcoux's 19 books
at http://amzn.to/ZiCTRj

Special Offer Just for Readers of this Book:

Contact Tom Marcoux at tomsupercoach@gmail.com for special discounts on books, workshops and presentations. Just mention your experience with this book.

www.ingramcontent.com/pod-product-compliance
Lightning Source LLC
Chambersburg PA
CBHW072307210326
41519CB00057B/3046